Jump Rope Training

Jump Rope Training

Buddy Lee

Human Kinetics

Library of Congress Cataloging-in-Publication Data

Lee, Buddy, 1958-
  Jump rope training / Buddy Lee.
Includes index.
  ISBN 0-7360-4151-6 (soft cover)
  1. Rope skipping. 2. Physical fitness. I. Title.
  GV498.L44 2003
  796.2--dc21

                                                          2003000618

ISBN-10: 0-7360-4151-6
ISBN-13: 978-0-7360-4151-5

Acquisitions Editor: Martin Barnard; **Developmental Editor:** Leigh LaHood; **Assistant Editor:** Alisha Jeddeloh; **Copyeditor:** Jacqueline Eaton Blakley; **Proofreader:** Coree Clark; **Indexer:** Betty Frizzéll; **Permission Manager:** Toni Harte; **Graphic Designer:** Fred Starbird; **Graphic Artist:** Tara Welsch; **Photo Manager:** Dan Wendt; **Cover Designer:** Keith Blomberg; **Photographer (cover):** Tom Roberts; **Photographer (interior):** photos on pages 4, 7, 64, 93, 104, and 112 © Human Kinetics; all other photos by Tom Roberts; **Art Manager:** Dan Wendt; **Illustrator:** Mic Greenberg; **Printer:** United Graphics

Human Kinetics books are available at special discounts for bulk purchase. Special editions or book excerpts can also be created to specification. For details, contact the Special Sales Manager at Human Kinetics.

Printed in the United States of America   10   9   8   7

Human Kinetics
Web site: www.HumanKinetics.com

United States: Human Kinetics
P.O. Box 5076
Champaign, IL 61825-5076
800-747-4457
e-mail: humank@hkusa.com

Canada: Human Kinetics
475 Devonshire Road Unit 100
Windsor, ON N8Y 2L5
800-465-7301 (in Canada only)
e-mail: orders@hkcanada.com

Europe: Human Kinetics
107 Bradford Road
Stanningley
Leeds LS28 6AT, United Kingdom
+44 (0) 113 255 5665
e-mail: hk@hkeurope.com

Australia: Human Kinetics
57A Price Avenue
Lower Mitcham, South Australia 5062
08 8277 1555
e-mail: liaw@hkaustralia.com

New Zealand: Human Kinetics
Division of Sports Distributors NZ Ltd.
P.O. Box 300 226 Albany
North Shore City, Auckland
0064 9 448 1207
e-mail: info@humankinetics.co.nz

This book is dedicated to all those who practice and endorse jump rope for health and fitness.

A special dedication goes out to my mother, Mittie Lee, a true champion in life, who inspired me through her struggles and triumphs in raising six children by herself. From her strong character and spirit I was taught important lessons that helped to shape and mold my inner champion. She inspired me to stay focused, believe in myself, and never give up.

CONTENTS

Preface   ix

Acknowledgments   xvii

CHAPTER 1

Get a Jump on Training   1

CHAPTER 2

Master Jump Rope Skills   13

CHAPTER 3

Use Proven Rope Training Methods   37

CHAPTER 4

Build an Aerobic Base for Endurance   57

CHAPTER 5

Establish Anaerobic Power   63

CHAPTER 6

Train and Compete to the Max   69

CHAPTER 7

Jump Rope to Warm Up and   75
Cool Down

CHAPTER 8

Gain Speed and Quickness   91

CHAPTER 9

Develop Agility, Coordination,   103
and Balance

CHAPTER 10

Boost Strength and Power   111

CHAPTER 11

Condition for Specific Sports   127
and Fitness Goals

Bibliography   149

Index   151

About the Author   157

PREFACE
A LIVING VISION

As a teenager, I had no idea that I'd one day be the official jump rope conditioning consultant to 25 U.S. Olympic teams, be recognized as the leading jump rope conditioning expert in the United States, or perform more than 4,000 jump rope demonstrations in 30 countries. I didn't know that I would help design and patent a unique jump rope product and develop a fitness and sports training system used by millions of people around the world. I never dreamed the U.S. Figure Skating Association would make my jump rope training their number-one off-ice conditioning technique for all levels of skaters.

Ice skater Sarah Hughes, 2002 Olympic gold medalist, ordered my jump ropes for her off-ice training. Legendary basketball player Nancy Lieberman flew me to Texas to train her with the ropes before she tried out for the WNBA at age 38. When she later became the coach of the Detroit Shock, she implemented my jump rope training system for her players. USA Boxing also invited me to perform my rope show for "the Greatest," Muhammad Ali, at his World Cup Boxing Classic in Louisville, Kentucky. Hearing him say "Man, you are the greatest jumper I have ever seen" is a memory I'll always cherish. In addition, I had the privilege of performing for the president of the United States, being named the "world jump rope wizard" by the press, and creating Jump Rope Technology, Inc. All of my success has been a product of hard times, hard work, and good fortune.

My jump rope career started at the U.S. Olympic Training Center in Colorado Springs, one night after wrestling practice in 1986. My friend Gene Mills, world wrestling champion and one of the nation's greatest pinners, had prearranged to enter my jump rope and me into a radio broadcast dance contest at a local club. He even checked with the club manager to make sure that it was OK for me to enter the contest with my rope instead of dancing.

I agreed to enter the contest, and to my surprise I won. I won $50, which I split with a friend, and I thought that was it. Little did I know that Tony Britt, the U.S. Olympic Committee publicist, had sent out a press release about it.

The next morning, when I entered the gym at the training center, I was surprised to find cameramen and reporters from NBC, CBS, and ABC lined up for interviews. All stations broadcasted national television clips about me that made my phone ring off the hook, requesting that I do my rope show.

Two months later, I was on a plane to Japan to do a national TV commercial advertising a sore muscle spray that earned me $20,000. I learned later that it became the number-one-selling product for that company. This was the beginning of my jump rope career, and the requests for my jump rope presentations haven't stopped.

I grew up in the suburbs of Richmond, Virginia, in a community called Central Gardens that borders the city line and is nicknamed the "home of the athletes." In our neighborhood, the cool thing to do was to participate in school sports and community youth leagues. The ultimate goal was to earn a scholarship and go to college. A few of the older guys and girls did just that, but there were not many of them back then. I also dreamed of going to college. But it was very tough being raised by a single mom—money was tight and each day was a struggle. I was the middle kid of six, so I had to fight for everything, which prepared me later for my wrestling championship rounds. There was Jesse, the oldest, who helped our mom and looked after us; Joe, who started working at age 12 and was also a martial artist, dancer, and songwriter; Cynthia, the big money saver and second in command; Brenda, the spiritual one; and the youngest, Jonathan, a multisport athlete with a technical mind. We were all so different, but Mom was the nucleus who kept us safe, respectful, and together as a family.

Unfortunately, I did not see much of my father, and the few times I did, it was painful. He fought in the Korean War and was once a preacher and a very talented man; but his mind, body, and soul were robbed by alcoholism. It was while watching the news that my family and I first learned he was killed and then run over by a car. This took place a few months before I was to compete in the 1992 Olympic Trials and Barcelona Olympic Games. It was a sad time, but I was happy that he was forever safe and resting in peace.

Even though sports were big in our community, as youths we were all still surrounded by the temptations of drugs, gangs, and crime, but I made a choice at an early age to do what I needed to do to go to college. At age 13 I broke away from my group of mischievous friends, became my own leader, and made a personal commitment to be my best in and out of school. I stayed focused and hoped I'd make it on good grades and an athletic scholarship.

I first became curious about rope jumping after watching my next-door neighbor, Herbert Rainey, a fourth-degree black belt in karate, jump rope every day as part of his martial arts training. He knew I had goals of becoming the best wrestler in the state of Virginia and told me that rope jumping would not only increase my fitness, but would make me quicker. *Quicker?* I thought. I was already quick, and the idea of becoming quicker really intrigued me.

One day, I begged him to teach me how to jump rope. He stopped his workout and showed me the two basic jump rope techniques. They seemed simple then, but I now realize that he had introduced me to the foundation of any jump rope training system.

I incorporated rope jumping into my wrestling training when I was a sophomore at Highland Springs High School, a school known for its state championship basketball and football teams. Rudy Ward was my wrestling coach, teacher, father figure, and true friend. He played an important role in my life, and made all the difference in helping me become the school's first state wrestling champion. He even flew to watch me at the 1992 Olympic games. After graduating from high school, other Springer wrestlers soon followed in my footsteps, and Highland Springs High School soon became recognized in the state of Virginia as a wrestling powerhouse. I vividly recall how rope jumping, pushups (I would use a deck of cards to work up to a total 1,000 push-ups in sets of 100s), sit-ups (up to 600), and running very fast around the schoolyard telephone poles, provided the basis of my strength and conditioning program. It helped improve every aspect of my wrestling ability. I lost only two matches over the next three years. I completed my high school career as a Virginia state champion, state champion runner-up, and three-time regional and district champion, with a final record of 90-5-1. This wasn't bad, considering I had started the sport as a 105-pound ninth grader.

Jumping rope, regardless of your level of proficiency, boils down to a few basic skills. After Herbert taught me the first basic movements, I wanted to master those skills as quickly as I could so that I could move on to other jump rope techniques. My first jump rope session lasted into the night. By then, I had spent five hours practicing the basic bounce and the alternate-foot step. That was over 20 years ago, and I haven't put the rope down since.

As I continued jumping rope, I discovered that it did more than make me a quicker athlete. It also developed my cardiovascular and anaerobic fitness levels, which was especially important after I joined the Marine Corps upon my graduation from Old Dominion University.

Rope jumping also supplemented my running and resistance training programs and made the difference in my collegiate, military, and world-class sports careers. Under the coaching of Billy Martin Jr., my main workout partner and a three-time All-American wrestler from Oklahoma State University, and head coach Pete Robinson, who was a good mentor, I went on to become a freshman team All-American and two-time NCAA collegiate All-American. My accomplishments extended to being voted most valuable wrestler four times, freshman and senior athlete of the year, and three-time most outstanding male athlete of the year. Ultimately I was inducted into the school's sports hall of fame. I ended my Marine Corps military career as a three-time world military champion wrestler, three-time World Cup medalist, six-time U.S. national champion, 1988 Olympic team member first alternate, and 1992 U.S. Olympian. As a testimony to rope jumping as a way to attain superior conditioning, I competed in the longest overtime wrestling match in American history, 19:58 (record held from 1988 to 2000).

Over time, I created unique movements that added novelty and diversity to my training and kept me from getting bored. My routines did more than maintain my interest—they attracted small groups of people who'd watch me as I trained. Many of them wanted me to teach them how to jump like I did. I gave a few lessons—no big deal.

As the crowds increased, the U.S. Marine Corps asked me to travel around the country during my off-season, in a series of jump rope demonstrations to promote its recruiting effort. I guess it helped that by then I was already a U.S. Open national champion and the Armed Forces national champion for my wrestling weight class, a title I held for 10 years.

This gave me an opportunity to travel around the country displaying what I thought were just routine training movements. Meanwhile, many wrestlers on the Marine Corps wrestling team were enthusiastic about my program. Before I knew it, many of them were not only jumping, but were becoming world-class wrestlers. Master Sergeant Greg Gibson (1984 Olympic silver medalist) and elite teammates like Lou Dorrance, Craig Pittman, Eric Wetzel, LaRock Benford, Keith Byard, and Keith Wilson, to name a few, all jumped rope for the championship edge. Rope jumping had also enhanced their quickness and developed their explosiveness, which is critical to wrestling.

Jump rope training also helped the Marine Corps team dominate the Armed Forces wrestling championships for almost 13 years, during which we won five consecutive U.S. Open national championship titles and produced a few world champion wrestlers. One year we were the national champions in two styles of wrestling and national runner-up in the third style. We were considered the most versatile team in the world. As I approached my final year as a Marine, I had an idea: Why not design a jump rope that particularly developed critical athletic skills? I had been jumping rope for more than 20 years by the time I designed my first jump rope.

Most commercial jump ropes had deficiencies that reduced their effectiveness. By the time I designed my line of Hyperformance jump ropes, I knew how to maximize the effectiveness of rope jumping. I realized that a good rope along with a good program made the winning difference. That was the beginning of Jump Rope Technology.

My athletic career, however, was still on the rise. I made the 1992 U.S. Olympic team and the future looked extremely bright. Coach Tommy Legge organized a homecoming in Richmond with family, friends, and all the wrestling coaches who influenced my career. He showed me a few winning moves that I used throughout my college career. Shortly after the 1992 Olympic games, I was injured in a car accident and later diagnosed with a bulging disc. That injury was extremely painful, requiring years of therapy. It forced me to hang up my wrestling shoes for a while, and my career temporarily ended.

Three years later, as the 1996 Olympics approached, I had another idea. Why not try to make the team again? This time I had a different agenda: to prove the value of jump rope training. Although I had to stop wrestling for a few years, I had maintained a high fitness level through my self-created jump rope program.

Early in 1996, I began wrestling training again, with the intention of trying out for the U.S. Olympic team. It tested whether my ongoing jump rope training had prepared me for the demands of world-class competition by going through the U.S. Olympic Trials.

I began jump rope training with a renewed intensity. I still remembered key wrestling moves and I designed my jump rope training to simulate them. Until that moment, I used rope jumping just to stay in the best shape that I could. It was my cardiovascular workout tool and, well, it worked.

With only three months before the final Olympic Trials, I traveled to the U.S. Olympic Training Center in Colorado Springs to train with some of the best wrestlers in the nation. Many of them were among the best in the world.

Meanwhile, several national team coaches asked me to train their athletes. Before I knew it, I was invited to practices and camps to train numerous Olympic teams. Several sports organizations began requesting not only my ropes, but also my training routines. So, besides U.S. Olympic teams, I've trained members of the U.S. Professional Tennis Association, U.S.A. Professional Skating Association, and a host of other national sports organizations. Bosön, the principal Olympic sports training support organization of Sweden, has been using my jump rope training programs for all sports since 1995.

At the time, though, I had no idea that my jump rope program and style would captivate the interest of so many people. On May 10, 1996, I entered my first wrestling competition in several years. It took place in Pittsburgh, and it was one of the qualifiers for the final 1996 Olympic Trials for Greco-Roman wrestling. The pressure was on. To my surprise and great joy, I won and qualified for the final Olympic Trials.

My fifth-place finish in the finals, which were held in Concord, California, was a major personal achievement. My primary purpose was to show the world the incredible benefits of jump rope training. I proved to myself that a jump rope training program could be designed to help an athlete maintain the high level of cardiovascular fitness required of their sport. But I still wonder what I could have achieved if I had begun my training a year earlier.

1996 was filled with an even greater surprise for me. Cindy Stinger, handball athlete and three-time Olympian and manager of the U.S. Olympic Alumni Association, suggested that my jump presentation would be perfect for the Champions in Life program scheduled to be held at the nation's capital. Bonnie Blair, five-time Olympic gold medal speed skater, and I were selected among Olympians from the past and present to speak at this event held specifically for the president of the United States. I was asked to speak and to perform a jump rope demonstration. The event was televised nationally and reported by major national publications.

The following week, the U.S. Olympic Committee selected me as the first official jump rope conditioning consultant for all sports.

Meanwhile, I continued traveling around the United States performing and speaking at business, sports, and fitness conventions, using my jump rope demonstration to set up my motivational speeches. Although the demonstrations may have been entertaining, the interest laypeople showed in rope jumping surprised me. I was used to training athletes, who generally showed the greatest interest in my training programs.

However, I later developed programs for fitness enthusiasts or those who wanted to begin fitness training. I've heard from many of them over the years. One of them, Mark Pizzi, wrote to me, "Buddy, I have lost 40 pounds after using your jump rope and program, and today I am the vice president of Nationwide Insurance." Mark was able to jump rope on a regular basis because of a great feature of rope jumping: its portability. Rope jumping doesn't require good weather, a lot of space, or a fitness center; it was something he could do even in his office or hotel room.

Besides training athletes and fitness enthusiasts, I have used rope jumping to encourage youth to find their inner champion to live their dreams. In 1993, I started Buddy's Jumping Buddies Club for the neighborhood youth, to skip them in the right direction. These kids have gone on to compete and win in national and AAU Junior Olympic jump rope competitions. Today, the Jumping Buddies Club is sponsored by the Department of Justice Drug Enforcement Administration.

Many of the athletes I've trained over the years have benefited from my program and gone on to win numerous Olympic, world, and national titles. Olympic women's basketball player Ruthie Bolton would give me a call while traveling during pre-Olympic competition to let me know how they used my jump rope programs three times a week. They were considered one of the most highly conditioned teams and went undefeated in pre-Olympic competition, going on to become 1996 Olympic gold medalists. Many members of that team became superstars in the WNBA, like Lisa Leslie, Sheryl Swoopes, and Dawn Staley, to name a few. I even had the opportunity to introduce my program to legendary athletes like Olympic gold medalist swimmers Jenny Thompson and Jeff Rouse (also a former world record holder in backstroke); Michael Gostigian, three-time Olympian and world record holder in modern pentathlon; and of course my Olympic wrestling family. The 2000 Olympic gold medalist and 2001 world champion Rulon Gardner strongly advocates my jump rope system. Today he is recognized as the first heavyweight wrestler to defeat Russian Alexander Karelin, a 10-time Greco-Roman world wrestling champion who had never lost a match. Rulon continues to use my jump rope as an integral part of his training and credits it with keeping him in shape; helping him maintain good balance, quickness, explosiveness, and focus; and enabling him to recover quickly from all types of injuries.

Other great coaches and athletes have used rope jumping to develop different athletic benefits as well. Olympic skating coach Audrey Weisiger uses it to improve agility and what she calls "efficiency of movement" among her skaters. Rope jumping enhances "efficient movements" because it demands a precise coordination of multiple muscle groups. Skating, like gymnastics, is often judged by aesthetic standards in addition to technical skill. Aesthetic standards put a premium on how fluid or how efficiently a movement is executed.

Another lay jumper, though, brought something to my attention. He is an avid bowler and I told him that he should consider jumping rope as a way to improve his bowling game. Jumping rope, in addition to increasing hand-eye coordination, also enhances hand-eye-foot coordination. One of the most important requirements of an effective bowling technique is to ensure one's bowling hand and the alternate foot reach the foul line at the same time. It's called timing. The precision of this simple movement is critical to bowling accuracy.

My friend vigorously jumped rope for a couple of months. His timing radically improved and he bowled three perfect games over a six-week period. He'd never done that before.

Over the years, I've received numerous testimonials about the benefits of rope jumping from world-class athletes and lay fitness enthusiasts. I've often asked myself why rope jumping works. I've read many books, studies, and other materials on the subject. This book, however, will combine the key reasons why rope jumping works with training programs that are particularly designed to enhance sports-specific athletic skills.

Rope jumping not only helped me to develop into an Olympic athlete, it eliminated boredom and made my training challenging and fun. It has vastly improved my sports proficiency and allowed me to reach heights I'd never dreamed of. Today I have joined forces with Elvis Malcolm,

15-time world jump rope champion from Toronto; Anna Sandwall, vice president and chief operations officer of Jump Rope Technology; Ray Tademy, Marine Corps veteran and technical writer; and Paul Feciura, director of Buddy's Jumping Buddies Club and co-inventor, to help produce technically engineered products and high-intensity programs that redefine jump rope for the 21st century. Our mission is to motivate, educate, and encourage the world to jump rope as a way of life. I hope you can meet the challenge of my jump rope training system and discover its powers. I am certain it will take you to the next level and help you reach your fitness and sports training goals.

ACKNOWLEDGMENTS

It takes a community of family, friends, teachers, coaches, business associates, and organizations to shape and mold an Olympian.

I thank Human Kinetics, especially Martin Barnard, Theresa Campbell, and Leigh LaHood, who helped to keep this book on track to produce a finished product. Thanks to Gray Cook for his support and implementation of my jump rope training system.

A special thanks to my team and family of jump rope experts—Ray Tademy, Anna Sandwall Lee, Paul Feciura, Elvis Malcolm, and Connie Lee—who have helped me to redefine jump rope through training programs and technically-engineered equipment.

I also want to thank the following institutions of socialization that helped to prepare my mind, body, and spirit. They helped to motivate me all day . . . all night . . . all week . . . all month . . . all year . . . to make my dreams come true.

The U.S. Marines, U.S. Olympic Committee, national governing bodies, U.S. Figure Skating Association, Professional Skaters Association, U.S. Tennis Association, U.S. Professional Tennis Registry, USA Wrestling, AAU Wrestling, the Wrestling Institute, Old Dominion University, Boson Sports Institute, Bethlehem Baptist Church, Highland Springs High School, Fairfield Middle School, Central Gardens Elementary, Central Gardens Community, and all those individuals who stood by me over the years during both the good times and the tough times.

CHAPTER

1

GET A JUMP ON TRAINING

The sports training potential of rope jumping has long been underestimated, and jumping has been used to its full potential in only a few sports: boxing, wrestling, tennis, and martial arts. Many coaches of other sports encourage jump rope training for their athletes but are not sure how to use it to meet the unique training demands of their sport. When done properly, jump rope training can lead to dramatic improvements in sports performance.

For example, home run hitter Mark McGwire, who was the first person to break Roger Maris' record of 61 home runs in one season, used rope jumping to develop the dazzling bat speed that gave him an extra split second to decide whether to swing at a pitch.

Dallas Cowboys running back Emmitt Smith uses rope jumping to stay light on his feet so that he can dart through slim openings between blockers and defenders.

Bruce Lee, a famed martial artist who triggered a martial arts craze in America, used rope jumping as a warm-up and training strategy to develop timing, balance, quickness, and speed. Meanwhile, who can forget posters, pictures, and videos featuring the amazing Roberto Duran, Sugar Ray Leonard, and "the Greatest," Muhammad Ali, turning the rope in images of power, agility, and grace.

Why Rope Jumping Works

Rope jumping requires the coordination of several muscle groups to sustain the precisely timed and rhythmic movements that are integral to the exercise. It's the coordination of these muscle groups that increases the athlete's capacity for *dynamic balance*—the ability to maintain equilibrium while executing complex, vigorous, and omnidirectional movements.

Rope jumping increases dynamic balance because the athlete must make numerous neuromuscular adjustments to the imbalance created by each of the hundreds of jumps per training session. These adjustments also force the athlete to balance the body weight on the balls of the feet, reinforcing the universal athletic position. The universal athletic position is a standing position of readiness which allows the athlete to react quickly in any direction and then move back to the starting position. In sports play this position also requires slightly crouching with the weight balanced on the balls of the feet and one foot placed slightly in front of the other. As in a basketball player's defensive position, the arms may be slightly extended to the side, preparing the athlete for omnidirectional multijoint movements (see figure 1.1).

Figure 1.1   The universal athletic position.

The reinforcement of the universal athletic position through rope jumping also increases the athlete's ability to react and make accurate changes in direction. Ongoing adjustments also increase an athlete's capacity for streamlined and efficient movements.

Efficient movements are especially appreciated by older athletes, who realize that proper technique allows them to conserve energy and employ it strategically. Also, efficient movements lead directly to *increased endurance*.

Much of an athlete's energy can be wasted by compensating for inefficient movements. Watch a tired runner's irregular gait to see a vivid example of this principle at work. The effort to compensate for inefficient movements saps the body of energy and diminishes stamina. That's why many runners are often coached to "hold their form."

There is only one right way to jump for better sports performance: You must train with the rope the way you want to move in your sport. Jump for speed, power, and finesse. Only high-intensity jump rope training produces the greatest benefits in the least amount of time for improved fitness and sports performance.

Furthermore, efficient movements can create a synergy between quickness, timing, and strength that generates power and explosiveness while also extending endurance. Energy conserved through efficient movements is available for improved performance.

Concentrating on maintaining the rhythm of swinging the rope and jumping over it facilitates subtle neuromuscular adjustments, helping increase efficiency of movement. The melding of mind and movement is an unspoken secret of how to use jump rope training to improve performance.

Elite distance runners focus on their pace instead of trying to distract themselves from the pain and discomfort of their performance. In a similar way, jump rope training, which includes the synchronization of several muscle groups, requires and cultivates an athlete's capacity to monitor training and performance.

Paying moment-to-moment attention to sports performance not only enhances performance, it also increases *maximal oxygen uptake ($\dot{V}O_2max$)* and unloads more carbon dioxide with each breath. $\dot{V}O_2max$ is the maximum amount of oxygen your heart can provide to your muscles during sustained exercise. The more intense the jumping becomes, the more oxygen is consumed to sustain the intensity. But there is a point where no matter how intense jumping becomes, your body cannot increase the amount of oxygen; this is your $\dot{V}O_2max$. This level can start as low as 91 percent of the maximum heart rate, or at the highest end of the anaerobic zone. It is also referred to as the red line zone and can be experienced in a short, intense burst of sprint jumping for 10 to 30 seconds. The more fit you become, the more you can jump at this level to match the high energy demands of your sport. Your $\dot{V}O_2$max, or anaerobic power, leads to central circulatory fitness and is the key to maximizing your endurance training and performance in sports.

By increasing dynamic balance and moment-to-moment concentration, and training the body to make efficient movements, jump rope training can develop the main ingredients of the competitive edge in sports performance.

Gaining the Competitive Edge

In most competitions, victory is determined by edges in time and space. Edges in time are created or exploited by *quickness* and *speed* and can be sustained by *endurance*. For example, I may beat you out of the blocks and be able to run faster, but victory will be determined by whether I

A jump rope training program can help develop the agility needed in fast-action basketball play.

sustain the edge long enough to win. Even in blowouts or performances of complete dominance, there is usually an achieved and sustained edge over time that leads to a large margin of victory. If I'm a step faster per minute than the rest of the pack, I can win a marathon by a city block!

Achieving and sustaining this edge is every athlete's goal, and it takes a combination of skills. For example, combining quickness with strength can create explosiveness and power. Adding explosiveness and power to timing can amplify advantages in quickness and speed. These factors work together to give you an advantage.

Jump rope training, then, with its emphasis on fine-tuning neuromuscular adjustments, precise synchronization of multiple muscle groups, concentration, and the integration of several elements of the competitive edge, can dramatically enhance an athlete's sports performance.

My jump rope training system targets the anaerobic energy system and helps the athlete to develop speed, quickness, agility, and explosiveness—key factors in gaining and sustaining that competitive edge. Specific programs are included to target each of these factors.

Aerobic and Anaerobic Training

Rope jumping becomes aerobic and elicits a training response in athletes when performed for 10 minutes or longer in the *aerobic training zone,* which is 70 to 85 percent of the athlete's *maximum heart rate (MHR).* But the greatest benefits of jump rope training can be achieved when it is used to enhance the anaerobic energy system.

Once athletes have developed proper jumping technique and endurance, their jumping sessions can be performed in the *anaerobic training zone,* 85 to 95 percent of the MHR, for 30 to 120 seconds at a time and at the $\dot{V}O_2$max for 10 to 30 seconds. Athletes can receive maximum benefits in minimal time from a jump rope program tailored to the specific performance needs of their sport. My programs target the anaerobic energy system to develop competitive advantages in the skills discussed in the following sections.

Speed

Speed can be defined as quickness over a sustained period of time. It's speed that allows an athlete to maintain and build on slight advantages in distance and time or to close disadvantages in distance and time. Speed can be increased and extended by forcing the anaerobic energy system to operate at progressively greater levels of intensity for longer periods of time. My sprint program in chapter 8 will increase speed by challenging the athlete's anaerobic energy system to sustain maximum anaerobic intensity for up to two minutes. This will prepare the athlete for the anaerobic demands of most sports.

Quickness

Quickness is best understood as reaction time. It's reaction time that allows an athlete to take advantage of split-second opportunities to act or react. This includes windows of opportunity to gain an advantage or to recover from a disadvantage. Because most athletic movements are executed through hand or foot movements, and many times both, my jump rope training system specifically targets quickness of the hands and feet. My sprint training program, for example, emphasizes several sequences of quick hand and foot movements that can be tailored to match the demands of most sports.

Agility

Agility is an athlete's ability to accelerate, decelerate, and quickly change direction while maintaining balance, body control, and speed. It's very similar to balance in that it forces the athlete to regulate shifts in the body's center of gravity while constantly changing posture. Most sports require athletes to move in multiple planes while simultaneously changing direction. My circuit training program in chapter 9, in addition to developing quickness of the hands and feet, enhances agility by improving body control and full control of the feet. Greater agility also boosts speed and quickness of the hands and feet and it enables the athlete to instantly assess situations and make accurate changes in direction while moving at high speeds.

Explosiveness

Explosiveness is the spark of force that triggers speed. It can be described as force plus quickness. Explosiveness is critical for athletes who must rapidly reach their sprint speed to achieve or sustain a competitive advantage, such as football running backs and wide receivers. It is also necessary for basketball players, who depend on bursts of exertion to leap for rebounds, block shots, and dunks. My power programs in chapter 10 are especially designed to help athletes generate and project explosiveness into critical movements of their sport.

In addition to these targeted training benefits, my jump rope training system will also develop the following:

- Increased wrist, ankle, and knee strength
- Conditioning of the back, shoulders, and chest
- Increased grip strength
- Improved posture
- Increased proprioception of the feet and ankles

Football players rely on explosiveness to give them a performance edge over opponents.

- Increased strength in the calves and quadriceps
- Improvements in vertical leap, lateral shifting, and start speed
- Stimulation of the vestibular system, which enhances balance
- Reduced stretch-shortening cycle, leading to increased speed and reaction times
- Fat burning through the recruitment of multiple muscle groups
- Improved concentration, which reduces energy expenditure and increases endurance

Maximizing Jump Rope Training

Rope jumping makes very specific demands on the athlete's mind and body. My jump rope training system maximizes these unique mental and physical demands. The demands include the following:

- Timing the swing of the rope with the act of jumping over it
- Maintaining a firm grip on the rope handles to resist the centripetal and centrifugal forces of the swinging rope
- Quickness of the hands while being light on the feet
- Concentration in maintaining correct jump rope posture and technique
- Sustained bouts of anaerobic activity, followed by short rest periods

- Simulations of sport-specific movements
- Simulations of the energy demands of an athlete's sport
- Establishing a system to measure an athlete's improvements in anaerobic capacity and training intensity

You should train systematically to derive the greatest benefits from my jump rope training system. My system consists of a series of steps that will improve jump rope proficiency and jump rope capacity, preparing you for sport-specific jump rope training programs that will develop speed, quickness, agility, and explosiveness (chapters 8 through 10). The steps are as follows:

1. Learn the skill of jumping and develop an initial jump rope proficiency (chapter 2)
2. Learn the 15 sports training jumps (chapter 3)
3. Establish a basic jump rope capacity to prepare for the sport-specific jump rope training programs (chapters 4 and 5)
4. Establish a baseline to measure anaerobic fitness levels before beginning training programs (chapter 6)

My system combines anaerobic conditioning with simulations of sport-specificmovements to generate dramatic improvements in sports performance.

It should take two to four weeks for most athletes to pass through these steps. Each step builds on the previous one in a way that leads to dramatic improvements in targeted athletic capacities and reduces risk of injury. Once athletes pass through these steps, they're ready for jump rope training programs that simulate sport-specific movements, varying intensity and duration levels to simulate the energy system demands of their sport.

Comparing Rope Jumping to Other Exercises

Table 1.1 shows that rope jumping performed at a low intensity of 120 RPM (revolutions per minute) produces cardiovascular benefits. For athletes who prefer to use rope jumping as a fat-burning program, the following information is provided as a comparison between rope jumping and other fitness or training activities.

Table 1.1   Exercise Comparison Chart

10 minutes of rope jumping at 120 RPM produces the same cardiovascular fitness as the following activities.	
Activity	**Time**
Cycling	2 miles in 6 minutes
Tennis	2 sets
Running	1 mile in 12 minutes
Swimming	12 minutes
Jogging	30 minutes
Handball	20 minutes

Because jumping rope incorporates all the muscle groups and joints of the upper and lower body, it has greater fat-burning benefits than most cardiovascular activities, especially those that emphasize only lower-body muscle groups. A 150-pound person jumping rope at an average speed of 120 RPM burns 720 calories per hour (see table 1.2). Calories expended are determined by body weight. Therefore a heavier athlete would burn more calories during rope jumping.

Jump rope rates a close second to running in burning calories. But when arm and complex foot movements are added to a jumping session, its fat-burning capacities are immeasurable.

To burn away extra pounds, athletes can jump at 120 to 140 RPM. Combining this exercise with proper diet and rest can produce a noticeable outcome in a short period of time.

Over the years I have trained thousands of athletes for fitness and sports training. Rope jumping as a training method is effective because of its ability to improve dynamic balance, efficient movement, and specific sport skills. This book will explain in greater detail how you can use jump rope training to enhance your fitness or sports performance by answering such questions as: *What is the correct way to jump? How do I develop my jump rope capacity? How do I learn different techniques? How should I jump for my sport?* I want coaches and athletes to walk away with a greater understanding of rope jumping and its important link to enhancing overall sports performance.

Table 1.2 Energy Expenditure by a 150-Pound Person

Activity	Gross energy cost (cal/minute)
Light	
Cleaning, light (dusting, picking up)	3.2
Sitting	1.9
Shopping	2.9
Sleeping	1.1
Moderate	
Badminton	5.7
Bicycling (10 mph)	5.1
Bowling	3.8
Canoeing	5.1
Gardening	5.7
Golfing (no cart)	5.7
Kayaking	6.4
Swimming (treading water)	5.1
Walking (3 mph)	4.2
Hard	
Aerobic dance, high impact	8.9
Chopping wood	7.7
Circuit training	10.2
Playing tennis, doubles	7.7
Skating, roller or ice	8.9
Skiing, downhill, moderate effort	7.7
Walking with a backpack	8.9
Very hard	
Cross-country skiing	11.5
Jumping rope	10.2
Playing handball	15.3

Activity	Gross energy cost (cal/minute)
Rowing, vigorous effort	15.3
Running (10 min per mile)	12.8

Adapted, by permission, from Blair, Dunn, Marcus, Carpenter, and Jaret, 2001, Active Living, (Champaign, IL: Human Kinetics), 179-182.

Rope jumping has worked for the Stanford University women's swim team. The swimmers love it because it burns fat. "Buddy's routine is fabulous," says coach Richard Quick, who was also the U.S. Olympic women's swimming coach in 1992, 1996, and 2000. "Swimmers spend lots of time horizontal in cool water, so they have more body fat compared to other endurance athletes. That's one reason we jump rope. It burns calories."

MASTER JUMP ROPE SKILLS

This chapter will help you master the skill of rope jumping so that you may develop jump rope proficiency. It will demonstrate how different factors such as correct jump rope form, good posture, and understanding the three rope adjustments are keys to obtaining the greatest benefits in 5- to 10-minute jump rope training sessions. Combining other factors such as surface, equipment, and attire will maximize your jump rope training sessions while also reducing the risk of injury. Wear clothes that won't impede movement; use surfaces that absorb impact while generating a rebound effect; and use ropes that facilitate quickness, speed, and continuation. Knowing how to properly store your rope can help preserve its life and ensure functionality and overall performance of the rope.

Surface and Training Area

The best jump rope surfaces provide rebound for the execution of the takeoff phase of each jump and sufficient absorption for the landing phase. These surfaces generate quick rebounds and develop speed, quickness, and explosive power. Avoid jumping on concrete, as it will increase the risk of lower-body injuries. Recommended hard surfaces include the following:

- Rubberized gym floor or mat
- Wooden floor
- Artificial turf
- Sport court
- Carpeted surface
- Tennis court (clay)
- Gymnastics floor (spring surface)
- Level dirt (baseball infield)

A soft surface should be used only after mastering rope jumping on a hard surface. Soft surfaces like exercise mats provide more give when landing and require more energy for the takeoff phase, which can help develop leg, knee, and ankle strength. However, athletes recovering from knee problems or other leg injuries can initially train on soft surfaces (such as rubber mats) and at the beginning limit jumping bouts to no more than 10 seconds at a time. Recommended soft surfaces include wrestling mats, judo mats, and well-manicured grass.

Once a proper surface has been selected, identify an appropriate jump rope training area that has the following clearance criteria. (See also figure 2.1.)

Figure 2.1   The jump rope training area should extend two feet above the head and three feet beyond the length of each extended arm.

- 2 feet above the head
- 5 feet in front of the body
- 5 feet behind the body
- 3 feet beyond the distance of each extended arm

Shoes and Attire

Choose a pair of cross-training shoes with ample forefoot padding, because jumping rope requires bouncing and balancing body weight on the balls of the feet. As a guide, wear athletic or training gear you'd normally use while practicing or training for your sport. Also note the following considerations:

- Do not wear baggy clothing, which can come apart, drop to the floor, or become a distraction during the execution of jump rope movements.
- Do not wear hats, jewelry, or other accessories that can fall from the body during the execution of jump rope movements.
- Always lace your shoestrings properly to avoid tripping and potential injury.
- Tie back or pin down long hair to prevent its interfering with the swing of the rope.
- Women should wear a good support bra.
- Wear head and wrist bands to minimize interference from heavy perspiration.

Ropes

To determine which rope is right for you, use my motto: Train with the rope that allows you to best simulate the speed, quickness, and agility required of your sport. A lightweight aerodynamic speed rope easily responds to directional change with minimum air resistance. Heavy ropes combined with weight training primarily provide upper-body plyometrics workouts but aren't effective in increasing quickness of the hands and feet. The best application of a jump rope training program is the development of speed, quickness, agility, and explosiveness. A lightweight speed rope maximizes these and other benefits of jump rope training.

However, unskilled jumpers who have difficulty coordinating the rope swing with each jump can choose to master the basic jump rope skills with a thicker, slower-turning cord that comfortably turns at 120 RPM (revolutions per minute) or 2 RPS (revolutions per second). Once the basic skills have been mastered, I recommend a speed rope made with flexible PVC (polyvinyl chloride) plastic that easily turns at 180 to 300 RPM, or 3 to 5 RPS, for maximum training value. PVC is the most versatile material because it can be designed to the proper weight and thickness to maximize the rope's aerodynamic properties, therefore maximizing the possible number of repetitions that can be executed per set. The training programs later in this book are based on this type of rope.

This point introduces an important principle of my jump rope training system: continuation. Continuation is the number of successive jumps between catches of the rope. Sustained periods of continuation maximize rope jumping benefits.

Ropes made of slow-turning materials, such as cotton or lightweight leather, may comfortably turn at 2 RPS, but are insufficient for helping athletes to develop speed and quickness. A slow-turning rope also hampers continuation and forces athletes to compensate for the rope's drag through the air. This makes it more difficult to establish the degree of continuation needed to derive the greatest benefits from a jump rope training program. Speed and quickness can be improved when athletes are able to turn the rope at intensity levels of 3 to 5 RPS while moving their feet at the same frequency.

Be cautious of ropes made of cable rod material. Although these ropes can easily attain high rope speeds, this material poses a high risk for serious injuries to athletes and bypassers during high-intensity rope training.

Use table 2.1 to compare different types of ropes. I recommend any of the Hyperformance speed ropes because they have a patented external swivel ball bearing system that virtually eliminates the friction, drag, and wear present in other jump ropes, allowing ultra-fast turning action, omnidirectional movement, and better control for improved hand and foot speed. The total weight of the rope and handle is designed for a perfect fit and feel for both children and adults.

A Hyperformance rope's swivel ball bearing wrench secures and replaces the swivel bearings to optimize the rope's performance. The innovative adjustment system enables the athlete to adjust the rope to his or her height in seconds by cutting the cord to the desired length and twisting it back into the handle. The adjustment system also allows easy replacement of the rope cord. The aerodynamic rope cord has a balanced weight and helps control the rope swing, making it easy to master the skill of jumping. The swivel bearings, rope cords, and foam grips are replaceable. Remember, a training program is no good without good equipment.

"Buddy's ropes turn so quickly that you are forced to move your feet and hands much faster than you would using a conventional rope. This enhances agility and cardiovascular conditioning, and is great fun. If it wasn't the very best equipment I have used, I wouldn't recommend it," says Burton Richardson, leading authority on Bruce Lee's Jeet Kune Do concepts

Table 2.1 Rope Comparison Chart

Rope type	Performance
Leather rope	The leather rope has been around for at least 90 years and is well known in the boxing world. It does turn more efficiently than beaded, nylon, cotton, and heavy ropes but it does not compare to a speed rope in producing lightning-fast reflexes. Too much energy is wasted on the effort to turn the rope. This energy should be concentrated on foot speed. The leather rope is not adjustable, so the athlete is forced to either make wide circles with the wrists to compensate for the extra rope length, or crouch over to accommodate a rope that's too short. This promotes bad form and increases risk of injury. If you are using a leather rope, try to buy it in a size that is close to your ideal rope length. (This is the recommendation for all ropes that cannot be adjusted.)
Licorice speed rope	This thick-cord PVC rope is a good basic speed rope for learning the skill of jumping. While it offers sufficient rope speeds, it is not fast enough to improve reflexes for competitive advantage. This rope is not adjustable but can be shortened by tying knots by the handles.
Cable rope	Ropes made with cable can turn very fast, especially ropes made of thin, woven cable rod. They can be used only for speed jumping, not arm-cross movements or advanced jumping. Cable ropes are not very elastic, so they break easily. The cable rope is not adjustable and poses the greatest risk of injury to self and others when the jumper misses while jumping at high speeds.
Beaded rope	The beaded rope consists of plastic segmented links threaded onto a thin cotton cord. This hard plastic rope is common in elementary schools and is designed for outdoor jumping on cement. Depending on the heaviness of the beads, it can provide a good, even weight for helping athletes safely start jumping. However, it will not improve hand or foot speed. These ropes become hazardous when the rope cord gets worn and breaks, which causes the segmented parts to fly in all directions. You can sometimes adjust a rope cord by tediously untying a small knot in the handle and removing the necessary beads, then cutting the rope and tying a new knot.

(continued)

Table 2.1 *(continued)*

Cotton or nylon rope	Cotton and nylon ropes are made of the slowest-turning materials. These materials turn very poorly and create excessive drag. Therefore, they are not functional for sports cross-training. Regardless of how quickly you turn your wrists, these ropes won't respond fast enough to benefit any athlete in training. They are usually not adjustable and are the most inefficient of all ropes.
Heavy rope	Heavy ropes are commonly thought to help develop upper-body strength. However, if an athlete is an unskilled jumper, the heavy ropes cause too much stress on the body and injuries can occur from improper turning. Resistance training and calisthenics are safer and more effective ways to develop upper-body strength. A medicine ball also provides good plyometrics exercises for the upper body. A heavy rope is not adjustable and will not improve hand or foot speed.

Hyperformance swivel ball bearing speed ropes

Aero speed	This short-handle rope is suitable for all-out speed and power jumping. It is recommended for adults and children 13 and older.
Rope master	This long-handle rope can be used for speed and power, as well as intricate skills, such as arm, leg, and body crosses. It is recommended for adults and children 13 and older.
Junior speed	This short-handle rope is well suited for smaller hands, especially petite adults and kids age 6 to 12.

and *Inside Kung-Fu* magazine columnist. For more information on Hyperformance jump rope equipment, see www.buddyleejumpropes.com.

Rope Care

Another way to maximize your training benefits is to care for your rope. First, store it properly after each training session. Leaving your rope in very hot or cold temperatures can break or alter the shape of the PVC rope material. Second, let the rope hang from a hook, a door, or a coat rack, for example, when not in use. Wrapping the rope around its handles will create tangles that won't straighten until after thousands of revolutions. This can waste time, negatively influence your training, and reduce the training life of the rope.

Rope Measurements

There are three rope measurements for maximizing training benefits. The ideal rope length will originate from the standard rope measurement. As you become more proficient at jumping and better conditioned, shortening the rope can help produce even greater benefits. The need to challenge the body and stimulate increased recruitment of muscle fibers will be critical to achieving the competitive edge in sports performance.

A shorter rope leaves little room for error and forces the hands and feet to move faster, dramatically increasing rotational speeds. It will also increase whole-body awareness, lightning-fast reflexes, and rapid reaction times. These benefits often produce advantages that can make the winning difference in the championship round!

Rope Care

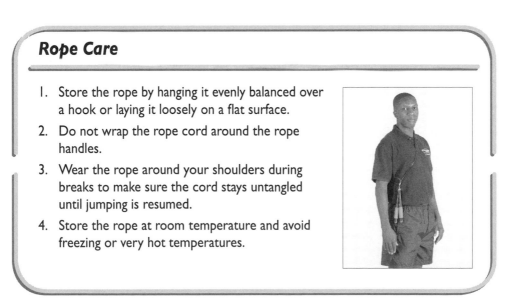

1. Store the rope by hanging it evenly balanced over a hook or laying it loosely on a flat surface.
2. Do not wrap the rope cord around the rope handles.
3. Wear the rope around your shoulders during breaks to make sure the cord stays untangled until jumping is resumed.
4. Store the rope at room temperature and avoid freezing or very hot temperatures.

The three suggested lengths I'll discuss here are established for sports cross-training. They are safe and comfortable for athletes who need to increase training intensity levels, which will increase foot speed, conditioning, and reflexes (reaction time). Keep in mind that correct jump rope form and technique are of paramount importance to achieving these rope speeds.

Standard Measurement

Measuring from the foot to the shoulder is ideal for mastering the 15 basic jumping techniques and can produce up to 200 RPM or 3.3 RPS.

Provided that the athlete has good jump rope form and posture, a rope adjusted at shoulder height will clear the head by at least 10 inches during the execution of basic jump rope movements (see figure 2.2). As athletes become more proficient the length of the rope can be reduced so that it clears the head by 3 to 6 inches during high-speed jump rope training sessions.

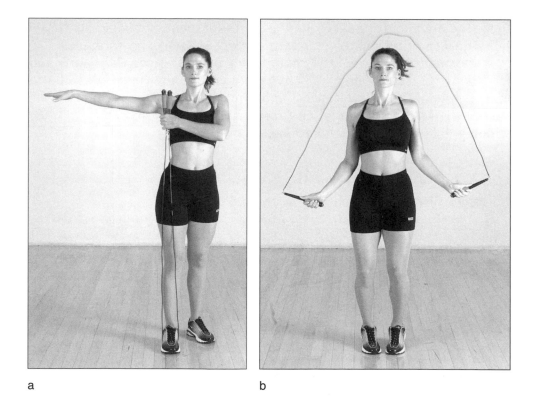

a   b

Figure 2.2   (a) For the standard measurement, extend the rope to the shoulder. (b) Rope clearance with the standard measurement.

To determine proper rope length, follow these steps.

1. Stand on the center of the rope with one foot.
2. Pull handles up along the side of your body so that the tips of the handles extend no higher than your shoulder (see figure 2.2a).

If the rope excessively smacks the surface with each pass or clears your head by more than a foot, it could be too long. Remember that the standard length is a guideline, not an exact measurement for all individuals.

If the handles extend beyond your shoulders, the rope is too long. This results in excessive drag through the air and reduces the rotational speed of the rope while increasing the frequency of catches and tangles. It also reduces duration, even for lightweight speed ropes.

Adjust the length by temporarily tying knots in the rope. Tying more than one knot on each side may affect jump rope efficiency, but proper rope length is preferable to maximal efficiency.

After becoming comfortable with the proper rope length, take out the knots and make a permanent adjustment to the rope length that's appropriate for your height. This will maximize the benefits you'll receive from your jump rope training. You can always shorten your rope again, so be careful when sizing it permanently to avoid cutting it too short.

Chest Measurement

Experienced jumpers can start with a shorter rope, one that extends from their feet to the upper-chest area when standing on the rope with one foot (see figure 2.3). This rope measurement is best for producing faster feet and hands and can produce speeds up to 5 RPS.

Lower Rib Cage Measurement

A rope that extends from the feet to the bottom of the rib cage creates the fastest jump rope speeds for sports cross-training without sacrificing proper body posture and good technique (see figure 2.4).

Adjusting the rope any lower so that it reaches the hips or belly button approaches the measurement used by competitive and world-class jumpers. This length should be avoided because it compromises correct jump rope form. It will take many years of training to safely jump with a rope at this level. Remember, you are not preparing for jump rope competitions. Our emphasis is on cross-training effectively with the jump rope at different rope lengths to develop a well-trained cardiovascular system and improve athletic skills and capacities.

Figure 2.3 Chest measurement.

a   b

Figure 2.4 (a) Lower rib cage measurement. (b) Rope clearance with the lower rib cage measurement.

Body Position

Stand upright with your head positioned squarely on your shoulders, your eyes focusing straight ahead. Your knees should be slightly bent and your feet should be placed no wider than shoulder-width apart with your body weight gently balanced on the balls of your feet (see figure 2.5). This is a natural position before taking any type of standing jump. In addition to reinforcing the position of readiness to react quickly in all directions, rope jumping will also have a positive effect on posture.

You may be able to run or walk with your back tilted forward or backward, but this won't work while making a series of successive jumps. An unbalanced starting position can result in a waste of energy as you try to reestablish the balance necessary for successive jumps. An unbalanced starting position also increases the potential for injury.

An upright, balanced posture allows you to execute jumping movements without wasting energy or causing excessive stress on the muscles and joints. This is a key to jumping rope for long durations.

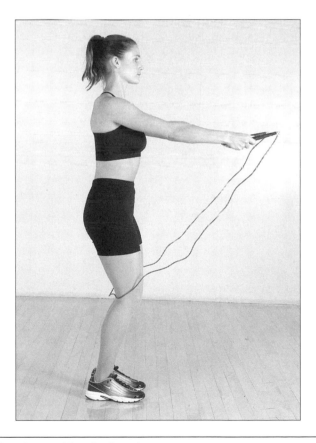

Figure 2.5   Starting position for jumping.

Proper Grip

Be sure the rope has a handle that you can comfortably grip with your thumb, index, and third fingers of each hand. Never grip the handles by holding them tightly in the hands. This will force you to use excessive movements to turn the rope and can cause hand, wrist, and arm injuries.

Keep the following points in mind while establishing correct grip (see figure 2.6).

1. Grip the handle with your thumb and index finger on the foam grip or at the center of the handle.
2. Wrap your hand around the handle.
3. Maintain a comfortable but firm grip. Never grip the jump rope handles too tightly.
4. Turn the rope, making 2-inch circles with the wrists.
5. Extend arms close to your sides, at about waist height. Keep rope handles parallel with the jumping surface.

By making small circular movements with the wrists to turn the rope, you will contribute to fine motor skill development of the wrists, fingers, and hands while improving grip strength. The correct grip will also minimize stress to the wrist and hands and increase jump rope proficiency. It will allow you to hold any size rope handle with control and comfort.

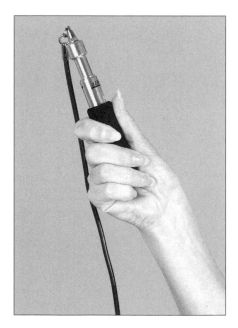

Figure 2.6 Proper rope grip.

Shadow Jumping

Shadow jumping is a simulation of rope jumping without the rope. This can help develop the proper jump rope form by teaching athletes how to jump less than an inch from the jumping surface and land lightly on the balls of the feet. It also serves as a warm-up before actual jumping with a rope.

Shadow jumping consists of three stages.

1. Simulate the takeoff and landing phase of rope jumping without the rope, making small circular movements with the wrists.
2. Swing the rope to the side of your body in time and rhythm with each jump (see figure 2.7).
3. Rest the rope behind the calves and, with knees slightly bent, practice swinging the rope in a nice, even arc over the body (see figures 2.8 and 2.9).

If you're jumping properly, you'll feel a continuous natural jumping reflex from your ankles to your calves, quadriceps, hamstrings, and gluteus muscles. The feel for this reflex is unique for each person, so you must become aware of how this movement is generated in your own body. For some, it's generated by a slight push from the ankles. As your

Figure 2.7 Swinging the rope to the side of the body.

Figure 2.8 Resting the rope behind the knees.

Figure 2.9   Swinging the rope in an even arc over the body.

awareness increases, you'll notice that the jumping movement can be triggered by a burst of energy from your abdomen that can be regulated by your breathing.

> **U**se shadow jumping as an opportunity to become aware of how multiple muscle groups are used to sustain the rhythm of the jumping reflex.

It can also feel like a natural springing movement that starts with the balls of your feet, is sustained by the ankles, and is reinforced by a subtle push from the knees or the quadriceps. If your mind is open, you'll begin to feel how each jump is generated and sustained by the coordinated effort of your whole body. This experience will teach you why it's so important to maintain an upright posture while jumping. An upright posture allows the jumping reflex to be easily sustained and absorbed by the whole body.

Biomechanics of Rope Jumping

Jump rope training features hundreds of executions of the three phases of each jump. The *load phase* requires the body to be balanced on the balls of the feet with the knees slightly flexed. The *flight phase* consists of those muscular contractions that propel the body high enough to clear the rope with each jump. In the *landing phase* you return to the surface by allowing your body weight to balance on the balls of your feet, with the knees flexing to help absorb the impact. Efficient recovery from the landing phase through the load phase to the flight phase is critical to deriving the benefits of jump rope training.

Load Phase

Your body weight should be balanced on the balls of your feet, with knees slightly bent. This position prepares the body for the multijoint demands of jumping rope. Ideally, you should jump off 1/2 to 3/4 of an inch from the jumping surface. To jump less than an inch from the surface and land lightly on the balls of the feet is a controlled movement that requires concentration and a certain level of body awareness. It's relatively easy to "give it all you've got" when you are asked to jump or leap, but it's quite a different matter to jump with control. With rope jumping, less is more. The control required to jump less than an inch from the surface while also ensuring that you land softly on the balls of the feet is a whole-body movement. See figure 2.10 for a diagram of the muscles worked in this phase.

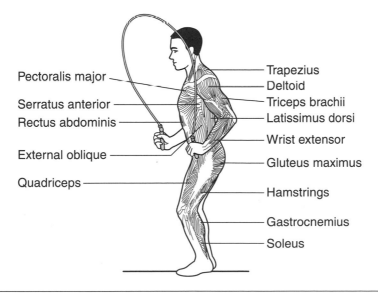

Pectoralis major
Serratus anterior
Rectus abdominis
External oblique
Quadriceps

Trapezius
Deltoid
Triceps brachii
Latissimus dorsi
Wrist extensor
Gluteus maximus
Hamstrings
Gastrocnemius
Soleus

Figure 2.10   Muscles used during the load phase.

Flight Phase

The flight phase consists of the *propulsion phase* and the *airborne phase.* Understanding what happens from the moment your feet leave the ground to when you are in the air is critical to maximizing training benefits and reducing injuries.

The propulsion is generated by a slight push from the ankles, calves, knees, and hips. Begin to push through the surface from the balls of the feet while pointing your toes downward as you lift into the air. This helps to strengthen the entire foot as your body becomes airborne (see figure 2.11a).

During the airborne phase the feet should rise about an inch from the surface as the rope passes under the feet. Swinging the rope and jumping over it recruits muscles from the upper and lower body (see figure 2.11b). This is essential to enhancing proprioception (the awareness of position in space) of the feet and ankles while increasing balance, rhythm, and timing and preventing injury. Repetition of these movements improves *kinesthetic awareness* (the body's awareness in space).

Landing Phase

During the landing phase, the shock-absorbing joints (knees, ankles, and hips) will help to spread the impact of each jump over a longer time and distance. It is the frequency of jumps that poses the greatest threat of injury to the jumper. Using proper technique and jumping on a surface that provides equal rebound and give will help to cushion the jump.

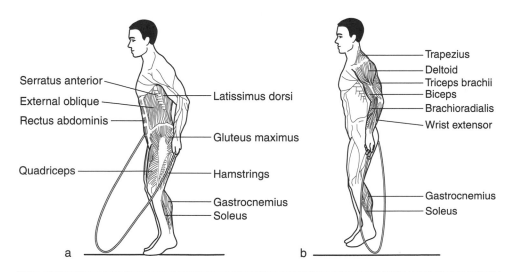

Figure 2.11   Muscles used during the (a) propulsion and (b) airborne phases.

The jumper must land softly on the balls of the feet, regardless of which technique is being executed. It's during the landing phase that the jumper develops balance while making the subtle neuromuscular adjustments that prepare the body for the subsequent load and flight phases. Jumping less than an inch from the surface while also ensuring that you land softly on the balls of your feet is a total-body movement (see figure 2.12).

The landing phase should be soft and silent, forcing the athlete to concentrate on perfect balance and the delicate placing of the feet with each jump. The heels should not touch. If the heels hit the floor or the feet land with an emphatic slap, an improper technique is being executed and the jumper risks injury and reduces training benefits. Concentration is required to ensure that contact with the surface is as short as possible, which produces less stress on the hips, knees, and ankles than jogging does.

Just as resistance training requires subtle adjustments from several muscle groups to balance the weight as it is being lifted and lowered, successive jumps draw on muscle groups from the whole body to reestablish balance and propulsion during each jump.

In many ways, rope jumping is like running. If you don't run with proper form, you risk early fatigue and injury. Good form allows you to maximize the benefits of the exercise and reduce the risk of injury. Managing the multiple movements required of a proper rope jumping form produces not only aerobic and anaerobic training effects, but develops the kinesthetic sense that will enhance balance, rhythm, and timing, producing graceful movement.

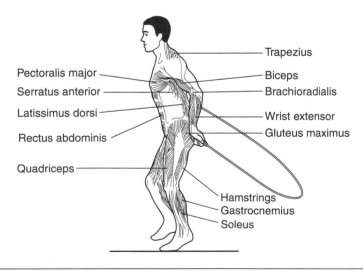

Figure 2.12   Muscles used during the landing phase.

The Two Basic Techniques

The *bounce step* and *alternate-foot step* are two basic jump rope techniques that will help you develop the proficiency necessary to use jump rope training to improve sports performance. In addition, these techniques will improve your conditioning level and create the muscle memory necessary to master the complex movements of other techniques.

These movements reinforce the proper jump rope training form, such as keeping an upright posture with the head squarely on the shoulders and the eyes facing ahead (which maintains balance); beginning the jump when the rope reaches the top of the head; and becoming aware of the stretch-shortening cycle that is a critical part of each jump.

The bounce and alternate-foot step are the best techniques to use to establish training baselines and to test conditioning and proficiency.

BOUNCE STEP

The bounce step is simple and effective. Time the swing of the rope while jumping with both feet.

PROCEDURE

1. Jump with your feet together.
2. Jump just high enough to clear the rope (1 inch off the ground) by pushing from the balls of the feet, slightly bending the knees and flexing the ankles.
3. Land lightly on the balls of your feet.
4. Stay on the balls of your feet and reload to repeat steps 2 and 3.

TECHNIQUE TIPS

- Bounce only once per swing of the rope—don't double-bounce.
- Begin with one jump at a time to establish timing and rhythm, then increase to 5 jumps per set.
- Master the bounce step before attempting the alternate-foot step.

BENEFITS

- Improves quickness, along with lightness of the feet

ALTERNATE-FOOT STEP

This is a similar movement to the bounce step. But instead of jumping with two feet, alternate jumping between both feet, as if running in place. Jump a little higher than an inch from the surface. Jump by lifting the knees forward *without kicking the feet backward*. Kicking the feet behind you while executing this technique will cause your feet to catch on the rope.

PROCEDURE

1. Swing the rope around and jump over it with one foot. From this position, on the second turn of the rope jump over it with the alternate foot.
2. Continue alternating feet (lifting knees as if jogging in place) at a slow pace until you establish a comfortable jumping rhythm.
3. Count only the right foot and multiply by two to get the total number of jumps.

TECHNIQUE TIPS

- Do not double-bounce.
- After jumping over with one foot, be sure to wait for the rope to pass over your head before jumping over it again with the second foot.
- Quickly and gently bounce on the balls of the feet.
- Do not kick feet backward.

BENEFITS

- Develops a quick first step and directional change
- Improves start speed

Developing Jump Rope Proficiency

Rope jumping is a skilled movement that takes discipline and practice to master. The off-season is the time to focus on the discipline and practice necessary to master this skilled movement.

Don't worry about speed or endurance at this time. For now, it's important to practice coordinating the rope swing with each jump. As your body develops muscle memory and your brain makes the proper neural connections, your timing, rhythm, speed, and endurance will dramatically improve.

Meanwhile, be prepared for numerous catches and tangles of the rope. As your proficiency improves, so will your conditioning. As your conditioning improves, these catches and tangles of the rope will become only occasional inconveniences.

Initially, rope jumping can be a frustrating experience. This is part of learning a new skill movement. With practice, you'll discover your own unique style and rhythm of jumping. You'll learn how to best make subtle adjustments of posture, body position, and effort that will lead to increased proficiency and fitness. Therefore, as you learn this new skilled movement, remember to do the following:

- Be patient with yourself. It takes time to learn a new skill.
- Stay committed to practicing. Never give up.
- Practice jumping before engaging in sports activity.
- Use goal-setting to force yourself to make incremental improvements.
- Use visualization to mentally simulate improvements in conditioning and proficiency.
- Jump in front of a mirror to learn correct form.

Once you're able to make at least 140 consecutive jumps with the bounce step and the alternate-foot step, you've developed the *basic jump rope proficiency* and skill to begin learning the 15 jump rope training techniques in chapter 3. This should take anywhere from one to two weeks. My jump rope training programs in the following chapters won't provide the training benefits you desire until you've first also developed *a basic jump rope capacity* by completing the four-step conditioning program in chapters 4 and 5.

Injury Prevention

Although rope jumping is an underestimated training tool, it is no different from any other activity or sport in that there is always a risk of injury.

How to Develop Jump Rope Proficiency

1. Practice to master the two basic skills of jumping. Learn to master the basic bounce step before attempting the alternate-foot step.

2. Your goal is to jump 140 times without a miss for one set, five sessions a week.

3. Begin with 5 to 10 jumps per set for a total of 10 sets per training session. Jump for 5 minutes. Rest as needed between each set.

4. Gradually increase the repetitions for each set by 10 to 25 reps as timing and jump capacity improve. As proficiency improves, it will take fewer sets to reach 140 jumps per session.

5. Follow the same steps for mastering the alternate-foot step.

Most injuries that occur in jump rope training are caused by improper jumping technique. Injuries can also be caused by too much jumping too soon with too rapid of an increase in intensity. Remember, safety should be the first consideration of any jump rope program.

To prevent injury and muscle soreness during jump rope conditioning, stretch before and after each session. It's especially important to stretch the calves.

Also, jump on a good surface; wear cross-training tennis shoes with forefoot padding to absorb impact; and progress slowly, taking plenty of time to master the skill of jumping. Don't rush to learn the 15 jump rope techniques in chapter 3 until you have mastered the skill of rope jumping as outlined in this chapter.

In the early phase of learning to master the skill of jumping, focus on the takeoff and landing of each jump. Jumping rope consists of landing lightly on the balls of the feet, good timing, jumping just high enough to clear the rope, and proper execution of the rope swing with each jump. The body and mind must gradually adapt to this new training technique, which has an impact on the skeletal and cardiovascular systems. As the body adjusts to the unique physical demands of jump rope training, the risk of ankle injury will be reduced because of dramatically improved proprioception.

Mastering the skill of jumping by intensely concentrating on proper execution is the best way to eliminate risk of injury. This is especially true when increasing intensity levels during jump rope conditioning programs. When athletes don't follow the guidelines of safe and effective jumping, the injuries listed on the next page can occur.

Common Injuries

- Sore calves and shin splints are the most common injuries and usually result from excessive jumping during the preparation or beginner's phase. Jumping on surfaces that don't provide sufficient give or rebound, such as concrete, can also cause shin splints.

- Sore shoulders, hands, and wrists can result from excessive arm movements and from squeezing the rope handles too tightly. Grip handles firmly, but not tightly.

- Jumping too high and landing hard and flatfooted in the early phases of rope jumping can cause sore knees and feet. Jumping on hard surfaces can also cause these injuries.

- Although ankle sprains, tendinitis, and injuries resulting from stress fractures are usually caused by other activities, improper jump rope form can aggravate these injuries.

When an injury occurs, the athlete should rest and refrain from jumping. Ice therapy is effective in treating most jump rope–related injuries. Apply an ice pack to the injury with an elastic wrap, 20 minutes on and 30 minutes off. The injured body part should be elevated so that it is higher than the heart. Treating injuries in this manner will help to decrease swelling and promote blood flow back to the heart.

As in most athletic training programs, jumping rope requires that the athlete proceed systematically and carefully to maximize training benefits while minimizing practice time. Proper attire, equipment, and jumping surface will reduce the potential for injury. Mastering the basics and proper technique will lead to noticeable training benefits while preparing the athlete for sport-specific jump rope training programs. Meanwhile, a familiarization with key elements of the biomechanics of jumping will help the athlete better understand how rope jumping improves conditioning and athletic performance. With this knowledge in mind, athletes will be ready to make rope jumping a standard part of their training programs.

3

USE PROVEN ROPE TRAINING METHODS

Athletes don't need to meet performance standards while learning the 15 jump rope training techniques outlined in this chapter. What's most important is learning how to properly execute these new techniques because they will be uniquely combined in programs designed to dramatically improve specific areas of sports performance. Meanwhile, learning these jumps makes *great* demands on balance, coordination, and agility while requiring horizontal (forward and backward) and lateral (side to side) movements.

The significance of agility in athletic performance has already been discussed in chapter 1. In this chapter the significance of agility is heightened, particularly the ability to make rapid, well-coordinated foot movements.

Learning the 15 new techniques requires the application of the same principles discussed in chapter 2. These include lifting the feet less than an inch from the surface (except for power jumps), making small (one-inch) circular motions with the wrists to turn the rope, landing lightly on the balls of the feet, and all aspects of proper form. The 15 techniques presuppose mastery of the two basic jump rope skills, the bounce step and the alternate-foot step.

Athletes having problems learning any of these new skills should use the shadow jumping tips we discussed in chapter 2:

- Practice each skill (jumping technique) by executing the movements without the rope, imagining that you are holding the rope in your hands.

- When possible, practice each skill with a rope by holding the rope to the side of your body and turning it in a way that simulates your rope jumping rhythm. This strategy will help you develop the timing necessary to execute a new rope jumping movement without worrying about catches or tangles of the rope.
- While learning each new skill, focus on proper execution rather than speed.

Before moving on to the four-step conditioning program in chapter 4, it is recommended that you master the 15 jump rope training techniques and be able to perform multiple jumps without catches of the rope. (This does not apply to the power jump discussed later in this chapter.)

The sports training jumps can be mastered at two levels. Executing each jump with a single rope swing will amount to low impact and focuses on speed, quickness, and agility while requiring the feet to raise no more than an inch from the surface during each jump. By slightly raising the feet from the surface, the jumper must jump rapidly and often, thereby increasing the conditioning level and improving balance and rhythm.

Attemptingthe 15 jump ropetrainingtechniques before mastering the bounce step and alternate-foot step will increasetheriskofinjury caused by improper landing, excessive movements, and undue stressontheankle, knee, and hip joints.

Power jumping, on the other hand, requires the athlete to lift the feet up to several inches from the surface while making small and fast circular movements with the wrists in order to execute multiple turns of the rope with each jump. These techniques develop explosiveness, vertical acceleration, hand and wrist strength, and anaerobic capacity.

Performing the sports training jumps at both levels can improve overall sports performance.

Low-Impact Jumping: Level I

All of the 15 jump rope techniques, with the exception of the power jump, are classified as low-impact jumping. This type of jumping involves leaving the surface at heights no greater than 1 inch.

To count a repetition of a jump, think of each technique as consisting of at least two movements. For example, when executing the high step, first lift your right knee, then your left knee. For the purpose of understanding the jump rope training programs later on in this book, "one high step" includes lifting both knees. Another example is the side straddle jump. The technique consists of first jumping with feet together, and then shoulder-width apart. This constitutes "one side straddle."

HIGH STEP

This is the same as the alternate-foot step, except the knees are raised to waist level.

PROCEDURE

1. Swing the rope around and jump over it with one foot, lifting your knee up to waist level.
2. From this position, swing the rope around again and jump over it with the alternate foot, lifting your knee up to waist level.
3. Continue alternating feet (as if jogging in place).
4. Keep back and head straight and stay on the balls of the feet.

TECHNIQUE TIPS

- Bring knees to waist level.
- Keep back straight.
- Do not kick feet backward.

BENEFITS

- Works the abdominal muscles
- Works the quadriceps
- Develops balance and explosive power for single-leg pushoffs
- Develops the muscles of the lower back and gluteals
- Develops the hip rotator

SIDE STRADDLE

PROCEDURE

1. Start with the bounce jump (feet together) so the rope passes under both feet.
2. Spread the feet to shoulder-width apart while the rope passes over your head.
3. Repeat.

TECHNIQUE TIPS

- Start with the bounce step and incorporate first one side straddle jump, then two, then three before alternating continuously.
- Do not extend feet wider than shoulder-width apart.

BENEFITS

- Dramatically improves coordination and agility
- Strengthens inner and outer thigh muscles
- Improves lateral shifting capabilities
- Improves speed in changes of direction
- Improves center of gravity and stability

FORWARD STRADDLE

PROCEDURE

1. Start with the bounce step stance.
2. On the first swing, jump by shifting the right foot forward.
3. On the second swing, jump by shifting the right foot back to its starting position while shifting the left foot forward.
4. Repeat.

TECHNIQUE TIPS

- Shift your feet only a few inches forward and backward.
- Quickly shift one foot forward and the other backward at the same time.
- Keep your body weight balanced on the balls of your feet.
- Like all new movements, this one takes practice, so keep at it.

BENEFITS

- Strengthens the quadriceps, hamstrings, ankles, and knees
- Further improves quickness and balance
- Simulates sport-specific running or scampering movements
- Reinforces forward and backward movement
- Develops a quick first step, quick stops, and quick directional change
- Develops the muscles of the lower extremities and trunk
- Develops the calf muscles

SKIER'S JUMP

PROCEDURE

1. Start with the bounce step stance.
2. Keep feet together and jump a few inches to the right on the first rope swing.
3. Keep feet together and jump a few inches to the left on the second rope swing.
4. Repeat.

TECHNIQUE TIPS

- Move your feet only a few inches to each side.
- Keep your feet together and torso upright.
- The movement should resemble a skier's slalom.

BENEFITS

- Develops timing, rhythm, and balance
- Improves flexibility of the legs and hips
- Improves lateral shifting capabilities and bounding
- Increases leg strength

BELL JUMP

PROCEDURE

1. Start with the bounce step stance.
2. Keep your feet together and jump a few inches forward on the first swing.
3. On the second swing, keep your feet together and jump a few inches backward.
4. Repeat.

TECHNIQUE TIPS

- Move your feet only a few inches back and forth.
- Keep your feet together.
- The movements should resemble the action of a bell clapper.

BENEFITS

- Develops coordination, balance, and agility
- Strengthens the quadriceps and knees
- Builds explosiveness
- Improves proprioception of the ankles
- Improves lateral and horizontal shifting capabilities

HALF TWISTER

This technique is a preparation for learning the full twister.

PROCEDURE

1. Start with the bounce step stance.
2. On the first swing, bounce jump and twist the lower half of your body so that the feet land with your toes pointed to the right.
3. On the second swing, bounce jump and face forward by returning to the starting position.
4. On the third swing, bounce jump and twist the lower half of your body so that your feet land with your toes pointed to the left.
5. Repeat this one-two-three swing sequence.

TECHNIQUE TIPS

- Twist only the lower half of your body.
- Hands and wrists must remain extended at the sides of your body during the entire movement while the torso remains upright with the head facing forward.

BENEFITS

- Develops hips, trunk rotation, and flexibility
- Burns fat around the waist
- Improves shifting or dodging abilities

FULL TWISTER

PROCEDURE

1. Start with the bounce step stance.
2. On the first swing, bounce jump and twist the lower half of your body so that the feet land with the toes pointed to the right.
3. On the second swing, bounce jump and twist the lower half of your body so that the feet land with the toes pointed to the left.
4. Repeat.

TECHNIQUE TIPS

- Twist the lower half of your body from left to right or right to left on each jump.
- Unlike the half twister, this technique eliminates the jump while facing forward.

BENEFITS

- Improves quickness and flexibility of the hips and reinforces rotational movements
- Burns fat around the waist
- Improves shifting or dodging abilities

X-FOOT CROSS

1. Start with the bounce step stance.
2. Spread the feet shoulder-width apart (as in the side straddle jump) while the rope passes over your head.
3. Cross your right leg over your left leg before the rope passes under your feet.
4. Spread your feet shoulder-width apart (as in the side straddle jump) before the rope passes over your head.
5. Cross your left leg over your right leg before the rope passes under your feet.
6. Repeat.

TECHNIQUE TIPS

- Start with the bounce step and incorporate one X-foot cross, then two, then three, before alternating continuously.
- When doing the side straddle jump, do not spread feet wider than shoulder-width apart.

BENEFITS

- Dramatically improves hand-foot coordination and agility
- Increases proprioception of the ankles
- Strengthens the inner and outer thigh muscles
- Works the stabilizing muscles around the hips and groin
- Improves lateral shifting capabilities
- Develops a crossover step

FORWARD SHUFFLE

PROCEDURE

1. Start with the bounce step stance.
2. On the first jump, shift the right foot a few inches forward with the knee extended.
3. On the second jump, shift the right foot backward to the starting position while shifting the left foot a few inches forward with the knee extended.
4. Repeat.

TECHNIQUE TIPS

- Alternate shifting your body weight from one foot to the other while keeping the body upright and maintaining the center of gravity.
- This movement is known to many as the Muhammad Ali shuffle.
- Land lightly on the balls of the feet. Do not land on the heels!

BENEFITS

- Develops balance, coordination, and timing
- Strengthens quadriceps, hamstrings, knees, and ankles

BACKWARD SHUFFLE

PROCEDURE

1. Start with the bounce step.
2. On the first jump, extend your right foot back by bending the knee at a 90-degree angle.
3. On the next jump, bring your right foot to the starting position while extending your left foot back by bending the knee at a 90-degree angle.
4. Repeat.

TECHNIQUE TIPS

- When the right knee is bent backward, jump with the left foot.
- When the left knee is bent backward, jump with the right foot.
- Keep your torso upright and your head squarely on your shoulders facing forward.
- Maintain your center of gravity.
- The movement should resemble a low backward kicking motion.

BENEFITS

- Improves balance, coordination, and timing
- Improves range of motion for the knees
- Strengthens and improves flexibility of the quadriceps and hip flexors
- Strengthens hamstrings and gluteus muscles

HEEL TO TOE

PROCEDURE

1. Start with the bounce step.
2. On the first jump, hop on your right foot and touch your left heel to the floor in front of you.
3. On the second jump, hop on your right foot again, touching your left toe to the floor next to your right foot.
4. Repeat on the opposite side.

TECHNIQUE TIPS

- Stay on the ball of your right foot when your left heel and toe touch. Repeat with opposite heel and toe.
- Keep your torso upright and your head squarely on your shoulders facing forward.
- Maintain your center of gravity.

BENEFITS

- Warms up Achilles tendon to prevent tendinitis

BACKWARD JUMPING

PROCEDURE

1. Jump with your feet together.
2. Start with the rope in front of your feet and make a big swing backward.
3. Start the jump when the rope passes over your head.

TECHNIQUE TIPS

- Bounce only once per swing of the rope—don't double-bounce.
- Turn the rope at waist level.
- Make small circles with your wrists.
- Pull your shoulders back when jumping.

BENEFITS

- Improves posture
- Improves muscular endurance in shoulders and arms

ARM CROSSOVER

When performing this technique, I recommend using a long-handle rope for easier extension.

PROCEDURE

1. Start from the bounce step stance.
2. On the first jump, swing the rope around and cross your arms at waist level while your feet jump over the rope.
3. After the rope has passed under your feet on the first jump, extend your arms to the sides of your body to uncross (as if you're executing the bounce step), creating a wide loop to jump through on the second jump.
4. Cross and uncross on subsequent jumps.

TECHNIQUE TIPS

- Practice the crossed-arm movement without jumping over the rope.
- Do not raise your arms above waist level.
- Keep the handles parallel with the floor.
- Do not jump over the rope until you have learned how to create an arc that's wide enough to jump through on the subsequent jump.

BENEFITS

- Dramatically improves hand-foot coordination
- Improves timing, rhythm, and balance
- Increases conditioning in chest, arms, shoulders, and back
- Improves grip strength

ARM SIDE SWING

This technique is a preparation for the side swing to jump.

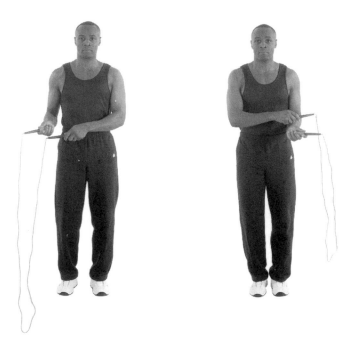

PROCEDURE

1. Start by holding the rope with both hands, waist high, on the right side of your body.
2. On the first jump, keep your arms together and swing the rope to the left side of your body.
3. On the next jump, swing the rope to the right side of your body by crossing the left arm over the right arm, creating a loop.
4. Repeat. Left-handed athletes should reverse the instructions.

TECHNIQUE TIPS

- Keep your arms together when swinging to the right and crossed when swinging to the left.
- Move your arms only while bouncing on the balls of your feet, as in the bounce or alternate-foot step.
- Bounce in place without jumping over the rope.

SIDE SWING TO JUMP

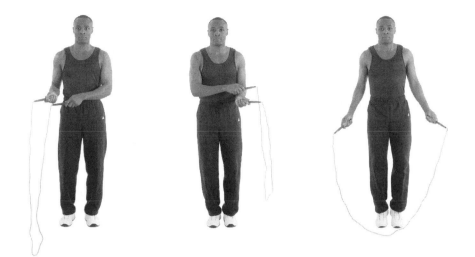

PROCEDURE

1. Repeat steps 1, 2, and 3 for the arm side swing (page 52).
2. On the third swing, open your arms to create a loop so that you can jump over the rope with the bounce step.
3. Repeat. Left-handed athletes should reverse the instructions.

TECHNIQUE TIPS

- Remember to also jump each time you swing the rope to the left and to the right.
- Execute each movement slowly until you get a feel for the unique timing and rhythm that must take place with each swing and jump.
- Gradually increase speed and intensity with subsequent training sessions.
- Take a few seconds to visualize the movements before each training session.

BENEFITS

- Develops hand-eye-foot coordination
- Develops quickness of the hands and feet
- Increases strength in the wrists
- Develops grip strength
- Works the shoulder rotators, front of chest, and back of shoulders

Power Jumping: Level 2

The power jump requires good form and is very effective for developing explosiveness. It is perhaps the most important and most difficult to master of the 15 jump rope techniques. The power jump is considered an advanced technique that requires more height than the other jumps, continuous explosive takeoffs, and controlled, safe landings. It requires more time to master than the other jumps and should be the last of the training techniques to learn.

There are different levels of power jumps: the *double (basic) power jump*, which you will learn here; the *triple power jump;* and the *quadruple (advanced) power jump*. Once you have mastered the first 14 techniques, they can be incorporated into the double or basic power jump.

Adding power jumps to the first 14 training techniques will produce greater training effects that enhance athletic performance. In order to receive the maximum benefits and to avoid injury, master the basic power jump before incorporating advanced power jump movements into your jump rope training routine.

POWER JUMP

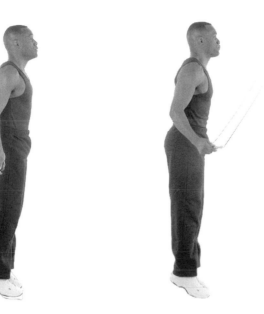

1. Start with the bounce step stance.
2. Execute three bounce step jumps.
3. On the fourth jump, bend your knees forward and push off. Jump at least 5 inches from the jumping surface while turning your wrists a little faster so that the rope passes under your feet twice in one jump.
4. Repeat.
5. When you have developed the rhythm and timing for this sequence, perform two consecutive power jumps, then three, then four, and so on.
6. Once you are able to perform 20 consecutive power jumps, concentrate on decreasing the height of the jump to 2 inches off the ground.

Perform the steps in three phases (see shadow jumping in chapter 2, page 25):

- Without the rope
- While turning the rope to the side of your body
- While jumping with the rope

- Keep your head straight and your torso relaxed to maintain balance.
- Your body should be in a straight line when taking off to jump.
- Turn your wrists with quick, small circles.
- Do not hold your breath.
- Do not squeeze the rope handles tightly.
- Use a rope measurement at shoulder level in the beginning and adjust to chest level when you improve.
- The key to power jumping is the quick turning of the wrists, not the height of the jump.

BENEFITS

- Improves explosiveness for vertical acceleration
- Improves grip strength and quickness of the hands
- Increases strength in arms, shoulders, and back
- Strengthens knees, ankles, and legs
- Improves balance, timing, and rhythm
- Improves anaerobic conditioning

CHAPTER

4

BUILD AN AEROBIC BASE FOR ENDURANCE

The importance of aerobic conditioning in sports performance extends to competitions today that were considered leisure activities in the past. The success of Tiger Woods in golf and Walter Ray Williams, Jr., in bowling has underscored the importance of aerobic conditioning even in competitions that don't require the levels of physical exertion required of basketball, for example, or soccer.

Aerobic conditioning is defined by how effectively the body uses oxygen to generate energy for long-term athletic performance. Anaerobic conditioning, on the other hand, is necessary for explosive athletic movements.

Although aerobic conditioning is most important for those activities that require sustained physical activity, an aerobically conditioned athlete can fare much better in activities such as golf, for example, than a less conditioned one. A competitive golfer or bowler isn't racing up and down a court or field, but is nevertheless engaged in activities that require deep concentration under stressful conditions. And it's the stress management benefits of aerobic conditioning that can give these athletes the competitive edge in their sports.

Several research studies have already demonstrated that aerobically fit subjects have lower levels of cardiovascular stress than those with lower levels of aerobic fitness. And once the stress response has been stimulated, aerobically fit subjects cope better and recover more quickly

Athletes concentrate best on complex tasks when they are in a relaxed mental and physical state. With increased oxygenation provided by aerobic fitness, the athlete will be able to sustain concentration for extended durations.

than unfit subjects. This explains why aerobically conditioned athletes often manage the demands of high-level competition more effectively.

Aerobic conditioning has other benefits besides extended physical endurance. First, the aerobically fit individual breathes more deeply than an unfit person. This results in increased blood flow and oxygenation of the muscles, even while at rest. This deepened breathing also helps trigger a relaxed physiological response from the autonomic nervous system that leads to poise, even under pressure.

Developing sufficient aerobic fitness levels through the conditioning phases of my program will help prepare athletes for the energy system demands of my jump rope training system. Insufficiently conditioned athletes won't be able to meet the anaerobic training demands of the circuit, sprint, and power programs.

Four-Step Conditioning Program

A basic jump rope capacity can be developed by a jump rope pretraining program that incorporates the following three principles.

- *Frequency*—the number of sessions per week to achieve training effects
- *Intensity*—the measurement of exertion in terms of energy needs, calories burned, and RPM (revolutions per minute)
- *Duration*—the length of time needed to improve aerobic and anaerobic conditioning levels

Athletes will have developed sufficient cardiovascular fitness and jump rope proficiency levels when they can sustain 5 (intermediate phase) and then 10 (conditioning phase) minutes of nonstop (without catches or tangles of the rope) jumping at an average pace of 180 RPM (3 RPS) as they pass through the four-step conditioning program by using a variety of jumps discussed in chapter 3. Achieving this *basic jump capacity* may require several weeks of commitment, conditioning, and training.

Athletes should engage in this conditioning program during the off-season, when there is plenty of time to practice a new skill and develop jump rope endurance.

The four-step conditioning program consists of four phases that have been sequentially organized to help the athlete develop a basic jump rope capacity in the shortest period of time. Developing this capacity will cultivate other benefits already mentioned in earlier chapters and prepare athletes for my jump rope training programs. It safely introduces increases in rope jumping intensity levels in a way that rapidly improves conditioning while minimizing risks of injury. The first three phases will increase aerobic capacity so that the athlete can jump 10 continuous minutes, while the fourth phase will help develop the anaerobic fitness level necessary for performing the advanced jump rope training programs. After completing the four phases in chapters 4 and 5, the athlete will develop a baseline to establish intensity levels necessary for the jump rope training programs in chapter 6. The phases are named as follows:

1. Preparation
2. Intermediate
3. Conditioning
4. Sports training

Athletes should move to subsequent phases of the four-step conditioning program only after meeting the performance standards of the current phase. Prematurely moving to the next phase may not only risk injury, but may also minimize the benefits of future jump rope training.

The time spent in each phase will be determined by the athlete's level of physical conditioning and how long it takes to meet the standards of proficiency. Well-conditioned athletes with rope jumping experience may be proficient enough to start at the intermediate phase. Other athletes with even more jump rope experience, or those who regularly train with a rope, may have sufficient conditioning and proficiency to tackle the conditioning phase. Unskilled jumpers or those at poor conditioning levels should start at the preparation phase.

Preparation Phase

500 jumps per session, 4 to 5 times a week for 1 to 2 weeks. Athletes should begin the preparation phase only after they've mastered the bounce step and alternate-foot step and developed a basic jump rope proficiency of 140 consecutive jumps for each technique in chapter 2. In the first few sessions of the first week, emphasis should be placed on reinforcing proper jumping form and raising the intensity level while alternating between the bounce and alternate-foot step. This is the first step toward developing a basic jump rope capacity as the athlete works to meet the following performance standards:

• Check jump rope proficiency. Perfect the two basic skills of jumping (the bounce and alternate-foot steps) so that you can easily make the transition between one skill and the next without losing rhythm and timing. Try each skill with four repetitions each before executing the next skill. For example, execute four bounce steps and then four alternate-foot steps while jumping an inch off the surface, making small circles with the wrists to execute each turn of the rope. By the end of the first week, you should be able to make 200 jumps without a miss. Next, try to reach 500 jumps in three sets; then shoot for 500 jumps in two sets.

• Eventually work up to a set of 500 consecutive jumps (without catches or tangles of the rope) while alternating between the bounce step and the alternate-foot step at a minimum pace of 160 RPM.

This phase will gradually condition the cardiovascular system and the multijoint muscle groups required to execute jump rope movements. It will also prepare athletes for the energy system demands, intensity levels, and proficiency levels necessary for the conditioning phase.

Intermediate Phase

5 minutes per session, 4 to 5 times a week for 2 to 3 weeks. During the preparation phase, athletes should have developed sufficient skill and cardiovascular conditioning levels that will allow increases in training intensity without risking injury. Meanwhile, the sense of balance, timing, rhythm, and coordination should have noticeably improved. With these gains, additional jump rope techniques from chapter 3 can be added to challenge and further increase jump rope proficiency.

Athletes will work to meet the following performance standards during the intermediate phase.

• Progress from 500 jumps in a set to 5 minutes of continuous jumping at a pace of 160 to 180 RPM while alternating between the bounce step and the alternate-foot step

• Add the side straddle, forward straddle, bell jump, and skier's jump to the jump rope repertoire

• Alternate between the bounce step, alternate-foot step, and these new movements during each jump rope set

For example, a set can consist of one or more minutes of jumping while alternating between the bounce and alternate-foot steps, followed by such combinations as the following:

4 side straddles, 4 forward straddles, 4 bounce steps

4 skier's jumps, 4 bell jumps, 4 bounce steps

4 forward shuffles, 4 backward shuffles, 4 bounce steps

4 high steps, 4 alternate-foot steps, 4 bounce steps

Repeat this sequence as many times as possible each session, using the bounce step as a transition between each technique, before completing the session with a minute or more of alternating between the alternate-foot step and the bounce step.

These performance goals are much more challenging than those of the preparation phase. The best way to develop this new level of conditioning and proficiency is to *gradually increase the duration of continuation each session until the goal of 5 minutes of continuous jumping is reached.*

For example, continuation goals at the proper intensity level (160 to 180 RPM) can be increased by a minute per session or by increasing the number of jump repetitions per bout. By the third week, athletes should have easily developed the proficiency and conditioning levels to meet the performance standard for the intermediate phase and be prepared to move on to the conditioning phase.

Although it may take up to three weeks for some athletes to meet this increased standard, highly conditioned and diligent athletes may achieve it in less than two weeks.

Conditioning Phase

10 minutes per session, 4 to 5 times a week for 1 to 2 weeks. By the end of the conditioning phase, athletes should be able to jump rope for 10 minutes at an intensity level of 180 RPM without a miss or catch of the rope. Meanwhile, athletes should work combinations of jumps from chapter 3 into this 10-minute routine.

Just as in the intermediate phase, athletes should increase duration until they reach this 10-minute goal. This standard of 10 minutes of continuous jumping is designed to ensure the athlete has developed a sufficient aerobic fitness level to tackle the demands of the sports training phase.

Sports Training Phase

The sports training phase is designed to increase intensity levels from 85 to 95 percent of the MHR in order to prepare the cardiovascular system for advanced jump rope training programs. The key to maximizing the benefits of jump rope training is to use it to increase anaerobic fitness levels. In the next chapter, I will tell you how to use rope jumping to improve anaerobic fitness levels in the sports training phase. Once you complete the sports training phase, you'll be ready to tackle my jump rope training programs, designed to push athletes to taxing anaerobic thresholds that will allow them to derive the maximum benefits for their sport.

The Story of Chess Great Bobby Fischer

Bobby Fischer undertook an unusual preparation strategy for the 1972 world chess championships. He swam, lifted weights, and ran daily in preparation for his showdown against Boris Spassky, the reigning world chess champion.

Fischer had studied Spassky on tape and realized that his prospective opponent made mistakes in competition only after becoming physically drained by the stress of the event. Fischer concluded that his superior physical condition would *give him an edge* by allowing him to remain sharp and focused during *the duration of the contest* while his opponent's physical and mental energy waned. The strategy was successful and Fischer became the first American to win the world chess championship.

It was Fischer's recognition of the mental benefits of his physical fitness program that gave him a competitive edge. For today's athlete, it's the recognition of the unique training benefits of rope jumping and the ways it enhances mental and physical performance that will be the key to a competitive edge.

ESTABLISH ANAEROBIC POWER

Aerobic training develops slow-twitch muscle fibers, which are used for long-term, continuous physical activity. Anaerobic training develops fast-twitch muscle fibers, which are critical for sports requiring quick, explosive movements. Fast-twitch muscle actions draw on a different energy resource than the slow-twitch muscle fibers that are trained through aerobic conditioning.

Aerobic conditioning develops the body's capacity to use oxygen for long-term energy production. Anaerobic conditioning trains the body to use energy sources in the absence of oxygen, allowing intense efforts for short durations. Using anaerobic energy leads to the buildup of lactic acid in the blood and stores up the glucose that prepares fast-twitch muscle fibers for critical bursts of activity at the appropriate time.

Jumping to Improve Anaerobic Fitness

Rope jumping for peak sports performance occurs when jump rope training is performed at 85 to 95 percent of the MHR (maximum heart rate). This is an intensity level of 180 to 220 RPM for most athletes.

Once athletes have developed a basic jump rope capacity in the first three phases of my four-step conditioning program (chapter 4), they can begin jump rope training sessions at the intensity levels necessary to

Track and field athletes can use jump rope training to develop fast-twitch muscle fibers for quick, explosive movements.

improve anaerobic conditioning. This can be done in 30- to 120-second jump rope sets at 85 to 95 percent of MHR. If properly executed, maximum benefits of jump rope training can be derived in 5- to 10-minute sessions three times a week, depending on the season.

In my training programs, athletes are challenged to execute as many jumps as possible in a short period of time, which should result in muscle fatigue and oxygen deprivation within seconds. That's because this explosion of energy temporarily depletes the target muscle's glucose stores.

To best improve anaerobic fitness levels, athletes should allow a brief recovery period after a set before executing a subsequent set. Initially, the athlete should rest one second for each second of exertion. As anaerobic conditioning improves, one can reduce the rest period to one second per two seconds of exertion. Supremely conditioned athletes can rest one second for every three seconds of exertion.

Resting is an application of the body's *supercompensation principle,* which states that the body recovers from anaerobic exercise bursts in a way that allows the body to execute subsequent sessions at higher levels of efficiency for longer durations. This training principle explains why my jump rope programs train fast-twitch muscle fibers for the explosive and quick movements necessary in most sports. After several sessions, however, the performance will taper off. This is why I recommend that athletes limit anaerobic conditioning sessions to 5- to 10-minute sessions combined with short 10- to 30-second sprints in the $\dot{V}O_2$max zone.

Although rope jumping for anaerobic conditioning demands high-intensity training levels, *athletes should never sacrifice proper form or technique for speed!* By slowly increasing both pace and reps one avoids the risk of injury and discomfort. In addition to increasing risks of injury, improper form and technique can minimize the benefits of jump rope training by allowing for inefficient movements, improper balance, and poor timing.

The best way to prepare for jump rope training for anaerobic conditioning is to establish practice sessions during which rapid jumps are executed in intervals of 30-second increments followed by 30-second rest periods. These sessions should be limited to 5 minutes until anaerobic endurance has been extended to 60-second sets (separated by rest periods of equal duration). Ambitious athletes can begin working on developing this capacity during the conditioning phase of the aerobic conditioning program. Here are some ideas:

- Do 15- to 30-second sprint sets during each training session.
- Initially, establish a 1-to-1 ratio between sprint sets and rest. For example, if you jump for 30 seconds, rest for 30 seconds.
- Work to establish a 2-to-1 ratio between activity and rest periods.

It's not unusual to experience muscle fatigue in the feet and calves during any phase of jump rope training. Even during the preparation phase of establishing an aerobic jump rope capacity, you can slowly begin to build on and increase your anaerobic threshold. As I've said many times already, jump rope training is best used as a strategy to take anaerobic training to the intensity level demanded of competitive sports.

Jumping rapidly for anaerobic training is quite different from the relatively leisurely pace of aerobic training. During anaerobic bursts, the body tenses as movements are restricted and focused through fast-twitch muscle fibers in the torso, lower body, arms, forearms, and wrists. For example, the swinging of the rope can become restricted to merely turning of the wrists, while jumping becomes a series of reflexive bursts from the ankles, calves, and quadriceps. After several anaerobic sets, athletes may become aware of other fast-twitch muscle fiber locations in the hamstrings, back, and shoulders. This involvement of multiple muscle groups makes rope jumping an ideal way to increase total-body anaerobic fitness. With this in mind, athletes should be ready for the final preparation stage before undertaking jump rope training programs.

Sports Training Phase

10-minute sessions, 3 times a week for 2 to 4 weeks. Once athletes have developed a basic jump rope capacity and learned most of the jumping techniques, there is one last test to determine whether they're ready for the jump rope sports training programs. This performance standard includes 10 minutes of continuous jumping at various intensity levels while employing all 15 jump rope techniques throughout the 10-minute set.

The intensity level in the sports training phase is increased to rope speeds of 220 RPM for 15 to 30 seconds at several intervals during the 10 minutes of continuous jumping. *This intensity level is the ideal standard for developing quickness and speed in my jump rope training programs.* Meanwhile, the intensity level should fall no lower than 160 RPM at any time during the 10 minutes of continuous jumping.

Athletes can begin training to meet this standard by structuring a 10-minute training period that starts with a relaxed bounce step (at least 160 RPM) while mixing in side straddle, bell jump, or alternate-foot step movements; increase to a pace of 220 RPM for 10 seconds before slowing back down to 160 RPM. Mixing in the skier's jump and forward straddle at varying intensity levels will further increase proficiency and conditioning. Incorporating these movements into your routine requires the high concentration levels demanded of my jump rope training programs.

How Jeff Rouse, Olympic Gold Medal Swimmer, Used Rope Jumping to Improve Anaerobic Conditioning

Jeff Rouse, a former world record holder in the 100-meter backstroke who won the gold medal in the 1996 Olympics, needed to add something to his training routine to give him the winning edge: a dry land training technique to improve his anaerobic conditioning *out* of the water. "You can only do so much hard stuff in the pool before it starts to get counterproductive," says Rouse.

Like all world-class athletes, he didn't have a lot of extra training time. I developed a jump rope training program that required 5 to 10 minutes a session, three times a week. That's all it takes if you train at the intensity level that matches the energy demands of your sport.

Jeff credited my jump rope conditioning system with helping him win a gold medal and set a world-record performance: "Buddy's speed rope is the smoothest-turning and quickest rope I have ever used. I warm up with it before lifting weights. It helped me to develop my anaerobic conditioning for the Olympic games."

When I served as the jump rope conditioning consultant to the United States Olympic Strength and Conditioning Program, hundreds of athletes, including 30 gold medalists, took advantage of the training benefits of my jump rope training system. These successes all began with the establishment of a good baseline.

Athletes should use this strategy until they are able to work all of the 15 jump rope techniques into one nonstop 10-minute set at 160 to 220 RPM.

Once athletes have completed the sports training phase, they're ready to move on to the jump rope training programs. However, athletes who primarily desire increased aerobic fitness levels can extend these jump rope durations to sessions of 15 to 30 minutes or three 10-minute sets with an average intensity level of 160 to 180 RPM, three to four times a week. These extended durations are sufficient to train athletes for the demands of endurance sports, such as long distance running.

CHAPTER

6

TRAIN AND COMPETE TO THE MAX

Once athletes have completed the sports training phase, they are ready for the next step in their jump rope training—learning how to train with the rope at an intensity level that simulates the energy system demands of their sport. An intensity level can be defined as the percentage of one's maximum oxygen uptake, the number of calories burned per minute, or the training heart rate. Another way to determine exercise intensity is to use a performance-based measurement. For my programs, the performance-based measure is the number of RPMs. However, in the beginning of your jump rope conditioning programs, use the heart rate measurement to understand and determine training effects or intensity levels. As you progress through my system, learn your body, and become more fit, you will outgrow the use of the heart-rate-based measurement and use the performance-based measure.

Establishing a Baseline for Measuring Jump Rope Intensity

Once an athlete has established a basic jump rope capacity and practiced jumping rope at anaerobic intensity levels, it's time to take a performance-based pretest to establish an anaerobic baseline. The pretest will determine whether an athlete is in good enough condition to begin jump rope training programs designed to improve sports performance. The pretest is a more appropriate measurement of training intensity than the traditional heart rate standard because the performance-based measurement captures the *physical* and *proficiency* demands required to derive the maximum benefits from jump rope training. Also, it is a more convenient way to measure training intensity and establishes a way for an athlete to set visual goals and mark improvements.

> *A baseline also teaches the athlete that the maintenance of a proper intensity level depends on a combination of conditioning, concentration, and technique. If one of these variables is off, the athlete will fail to reach the baseline.*

The pretest will ensure that athletes are training at the proper intensity level and become a standard method to measure gains in proficiency and anaerobic fitness. *It's a critical training benchmark that is based on how many jumps the athlete can make in a set period of time.* The athlete's goal is to meet or exceed this benchmark during each jump rope session. In rope jumping, establishing this baseline is like a track athlete trying to run a certain distance at a certain pace or within a certain period of time as a measure of training intensity or to mark improvements. As fitness and training proficiency improve, the athlete will set new baselines.

Regularly exceeding the baseline may reliably be attributed to gains in conditioning, concentration, and proficiency. As with any exercise, once an athlete's cardiovascular system adapts to the demands of physical training, he or she may be able to meet baseline standards at lower levels of physical exertion or heart rate training levels. Therefore, these athletes will have to increase intensity levels by jumping faster and increasing RPMs in order to continue to make training gains. In other words, establishing progressively higher performance-based baselines results in fitness gains. Once you are satisfied with your gains, maintain your baseline throughout your jump rope training programs. Depending on your age, it can take up to several years to achieve your maximum baseline; therefore, you can always stay motivated to improve your score.

Pretest for Establishing a Baseline

The pretest consists of jumping as many times as possible in 30, 60, 90, or 120 seconds using the alternate-foot step or power jump. The duration of the sprints will depend on the length of the sets in the training programs that you are entering. Table 6.1 shows an example of a 30-second pretest using the alternate-foot step. Take the average of the three 30-second sprints to establish an initial performance baseline. Table 6.2 gives an example of a 30-second pretest using the power jump.

Follow these tips on taking the pretest.

- Take the pretest on a training day *after* establishing a basic rope jumping capacity.
- Take the pretest when the body is well rested. The goal is to establish a level of performance that the athlete will be challenged to match or exceed in each subsequent rope jumping session.

Anyone who can exceed a well-established baseline on a consistent basis is making significant improvements in conditioning and proficiency. This may also be proof that one is increasing one's competitive edge. As the body adjusts to the unique physical demands of jump rope training, athletes will improve overall cardiovascular fitness and notice additional benefits:

- Increased reaction time and alertness
- The ability to exert more force while requiring less time to recover

Table 6.1   Pretest Example 1: 30 Seconds Using Alternate-Foot Step

Time Jump 3 times	Reps Record the reps for each set (count right foot and multiply by 2)	Baseline score Add reps of all sets and divide by 3
30 sec	50 jumps $\times$ 2 = 100	306 jumps / 3 = 102 (baseline)
30 sec	52 jumps $\times$ 2 = 104	
30 sec	51 jumps $\times$ 2 = 102	

Table 6.2   Pretest Example 2: 30 Seconds Using Power Jump

Time Jump 3 times	Reps Record the reps for each set	Baseline score Add reps of all sets and divide by 3
30 sec	40 jumps	126 jumps / 3 = 42 (baseline)
30 sec	45 jumps	
30 sec	41 jumps	

- Subtle improvements in overall balance and physical equilibrium
- Enhanced fine motor skill development of the fingers and hands
- Reduced or eliminated ankle injuries because of dramatically improved proprioception
- Improved posture and physical grace

If a baseline is passed even once, that new mark automatically becomes the new baseline for future training sessions!

Gains in proficiency and conditioning will be reflected in each new baseline. This means that the body is using energy more efficiently while making improvements in stamina. Both of these gains can contribute to improvements in speed and endurance. These improvements in performance may produce a justified rush of enthusiasm that will fuel your commitment to your program and help generate further improvements.

Target Training Zones

The chart below gives an approximate idea of the target heart rate training for aerobic, anaerobic, and $\dot{V}O_2$max zones. Once you develop a jump rope capacity, perform jump rope conditioning at the high end of the training zones for maximum benefits.

Aerobic zone	Anaerobic zone	$\dot{V}O_2$max zone
70 to 85% of MHR	85 to 95% of MHR	95 to 100% of MHR

It's possible for well-conditioned athletes to develop enough jump rope proficiency and endurance to establish a high baseline in a short period of time. This actually took place when I trained a group of junior skaters at the Fairfax Ice Skating Arena in Virginia (the former home rink of Michael Weiss, two-time Olympic figure skater).

I trained one 12-year-old skater to master the basic skills of rope jumping, jump rope training techniques, and the sports training phase outlined in this book after one week! He established a baseline of 100 jumps in 30 seconds, a level of proficiency and endurance that allowed him to immediately begin my basic jump rope training programs.

Finding Your Target Heart Rates

To quickly determine your target heart rate or training zone, jump for one minute at a high speed; stop and take your pulse for 10 seconds at the wrist, neck, or temple; and multiply by 6 to get the rate in beats per minute. In order to *calculate* your target heart rates, you must find your MHR (maximum heart rate). There are several ways to calculate your MHR, and most of them are inexact. It will take a cardiologist to determine your precise MHR. Also, several factors in addition to training and fitness, such as genes, can influence MHR. Nevertheless, a standard formula can give you a reasonable approximation of your MHR: 220 - age. Keep in mind that this measure may be off by 10 beats. Also, better-conditioned athletes may be able to sustain training intensities at MHR of people 5 or 10 years their junior.

Here is a formula for calculating your target heart rates once you have established your MHR:

MHR $\times$ 70% = target HR for aerobic training zone (low end)

MHR $\times$ 95% = target HR for anaerobic training zone (high end)

This chart shows an example of a 40-year-old male who used 220 - his age to determine his MHR.

MHR	Aerobic training zone (70-85% of MHR)	Anaerobic training zone (85-95% of MHR)	$\dot{V}O_2$max training zone (95-100% of MHR)
180	126-153	153-171	171-180

Performance-Based (RPM) Chart

Rope jumping can range from speeds of 140 RPM at the low end of the aerobic training zone to over 220 RPM at $\dot{V}O_2$max. As one becomes better conditioned one may reach for higher anaerobic thresholds to continue making training gains.

As athletes become better-skilled jumpers, they will be able to jump at higher intensity levels with lower energy costs. If this happens, there are a few things these athletes can do to continue making training and fitness gains:

- Vary rope speeds during each set and throughout each training session.

- Incorporate a variety of upper- and lower-body movements and techniques.
- Use all planes of the jumping surface while executing forward, backward, and lateral motions.

Though it is difficult to equate RPM and training heart rates, tables 6.3 and 6.4 can be used as guidelines. Keep in mind that it probably is best to rely on a performance-based measurement (by using the pretest) to determine increases in overall anaerobic conditioning, speed, quickness, and agility in my training programs.

Table 6.3   Intensity Chart Using the Alternate-Foot Step

RPS	RPM (right foot × 2)	Fitness level	Approximate target heart rate (%)	Suggested rope measurement
2.0-2.3	120-140	Warm up	60-70	Standard
2.3-2.7	140-160	Aerobic (low) 70-75	70-75	Standard
2.7-3.0	160-180	Aerobic (high) 75-80	75-80	Standard
3.0-3.3	180-200	Anaerobic (low)	85-90	Chest
3.3-3.7	200-220	Anaerobic (high)	90-95	Chest
3.7+	220+	$\dot{V}O_2$max (very high)	95-100	Chest or lower rib cage

Table 6.4   Intensity Chart Using the Power Jump

RPS	RPM	Fitness level	Approximate target heart rate (%)	Suggested rope measurement
1.0-1.2	60-70	Aerobic (low)	70-75	Standard
1.2-1.3	70-80	Aerobic (high)	75-80	Standard
1.3-1.7	80-100	Anaerobic (low)	85-90	Chest
1.7-2.0	100-120	Anaerobic (high)	90-95	Chest
2.0+	120+	$\dot{V}O_2$max (very high)	95-100	Chest or lower rib cage

JUMPROPETOWARMUP AND COOL DOWN

Rope jumping can be incorporated into an athlete's regular training program as a warm-up, active rest, or cool-down. The portability of rope jumping makes this possible even during competition. Exercise bikes and other equipment can require access to a gym or fitness center, while a jump rope requires only sufficient space and an adequate surface.

Rope jumping can be effective as a part of the active rest phase of resistance training, keeping the muscles warm while also activating fat-burning and aerobic energy systems at critical moments of the athlete's anaerobic training session.

Warming Up With the Jump Rope

One way to reduce risk of injury in all sports is to warm up properly before training and competition. Rope jumping incorporates all muscle groups, and it can quickly raise the heart rate while increasing blood circulation. There are three main methods you can use to warm up with the jump rope before sports play:

1. Jump to elevate the body temperature as a total-body warm-up to stretching exercises.

2. Jump as a warm-up to advanced jump rope training programs.

3. Jump to raise the heart rate as a transition into full-speed sports play.

Because rope jumping is a multijoint activity, it requires only a third of the time of those aerobic activities normally used to warm the muscles. This makes rope jumping an ideal warm-up to stretching exercises that prepare athletes for the training programs in the following chapters.

Although many coaches have recognized rope jumping as an effective warm-up to sports, they rarely use it as a safe and smooth transition into high-intensity sports activities. After athletes have learned how to execute my warm-up programs in this chapter, they will be able to use them as a transition into a full-speed sports workout from the moment they walk into the training site.

You may already do this without thinking about it, but begin the warm-up with a slow 1- to 2-minute prestretch to loosen the main muscles and joints used in rope jumping—the calves, knees, ankles, shoulders, and quadriceps. This important prestretch provides some joint mobility by improving flexibility of the ligaments and tendons and makes it easier to go right into rope jumping as a warm-up, cool-down, active rest, or transitional exercise. After the quick prestretch, jump for 5 minutes to raise the core body temperature, and then go into a more complete stretching session to prevent injury and prepare the body for more intense exercise. Stretches for this longer stretching session can be found on pages 79 to 82.

Procedures for the three methods of warming up with the rope are as follows:

As a warm-up to stretching exercises

1. Do a 1- to 2-minute light stretch.

2. Warm up with the jump rope for 5 minutes at a low intensity (140 RPM), using the basic warm-up program.

3. Stretch all major muscle groups well, especially the calves, for 10 to 20 minutes. Remember to hold each stretch for at least 20 seconds.

As a transition into full-speed sports play

1. Do a 1- to 2-minute light stretch.

2. Warm up with the advanced warm-up program.

3. Stretch all major muscle groups well, especially the calves, for 10 to 20 minutes.

4. Use the advanced warm-up program in this chapter (page 88) to elevate the heart rate to 85-90% of the MHR as a transition into full-speed sports play.

As a warm-up to my high-intensity jump rope training programs

1. Do a 1- to 2-minute light stretch.
2. Warm up with the intermediate warm-up program.
3. Stretch all major muscle groups well, especially the calves, for 10 to 20 minutes.
4. Do the sprint, power, or circuit training programs.

Active Rest With the Jump Rope

Rope jumping's portability and efficiency in time and space make it the most effective active rest activity to keep muscles warm and pliant between sets of weightlifting, during breaks in sports practice, or while waiting on the sideline in sports competition.

Here are some practical ways to use rope jumping as active rest.

- Between weight training sets, jump 100-160 times to warm muscles.
- Use the basic to advanced warm-up programs right before stepping onto the playing field.

I still remember how I would regularly warm up by jumping rope before each wrestling match, especially at national and world wrestling competitions. After jumping for a few minutes before my match, I'd end with a 10-second sprint to match the target heart rate zone I'd wrestle at during the match. Then I would wait approximately 20 seconds to let my heart rate settle before stepping on the mat.

When I stepped onto the wrestling mat to compete, I was a ball of energy and ready to explode, because my heart rate had already been in the target zone. It gave me an advantage over the competition and made it easier for me to score the first takedown without being overly winded. It also gave me the momentum to pin or superior-decision many of my opponents in the first two minutes.

At the 1993 National Greco-Roman Championships, I did just that. I defeated my first three opponents by a pin or by superior decision in the first two minutes. I had trained to win within the first two minutes because being the first to score in world-class competition often makes the difference in gaining momentum, and it ultimately determined the outcome of the matches. I credit my explosive energy and momentum to my unique and sport-specific jump rope warm-up.

Cooling Down With the Jump Rope

Cooling down after practice is just as important as warming up to minimize injuries. To ease the transition from full-speed sports play, use my basic warm-up program to gradually lower the heart rate. Stretch all major muscle groups well, especially the calves.

Stretching for Flexibility

Stretching is important to your training for many reasons, some less obvious than others. Stretching creates tension and elongation of muscle tissue and prepares it for activity. This stimulates neurological and circulatory activity. Stretching can also give you a great deal of feedback if you know how to listen to your body. If stretching produces pain in a muscle, you should get the area checked. If stretching causes discomfort in the joint and not simply tension in the muscle, you may also have a problem or you may be forcing the stretch. Learn to relax and breathe when you stretch. Use a moderate amount of tension when stretching and don't fight the stretch. Many who are new to stretching actually contract the muscle they are trying to stretch without realizing what they are doing.

You can also use your stretching program to check your symmetry. Most stretches are performed on the left and right side of the body (for the extremities) or they are done toward the left and right (for the spine); either way you have an opportunity to observe symmetry. If you observe differences, target the more limited movement and remain focused on the problem until it is resolved. When you jump rope you teach your brain and body to move with greater speed. You will learn to move by the way you train. If you train with tightness, you will move and compete with tightness. If you train with asymmetry (left-right imbalance), you will move and compete with asymmetry. The stretches on the following pages will give you an opportunity to look for limitation and asymmetries in your movement. With each stretch relax, breathe deeply, and slow down. It is best to perform the stretch on an exhalation. Hold each stretch 15 to 20 seconds.

Hip Flexor Stretch

1. Kneel with your right foot forward, left knee on the floor, and left knee back.

2. Lean forward, hips facing forward, keeping your body upright. See figure 7.1.

3. Bend your right knee, but don't allow it to go over your toe. Contract your buttocks under.

4. Repeat for the other leg.

Figure 7.1   Hip flexor stretch.

Seated Hamstrings and Calf Stretch

1. Inhale, exhale, and reach forward 6 inches above your left foot (so that your body forms a shape resembling the letter E). Lead with your chest, keeping your knee cap and toe pointed upward. See figure 7.2.

2. Repeat for the right leg.

Figure 7.2   Seated hamstrings and calf stretch.

Standing Calf Stretch

1. Stand with your hands about shoulder-width apart against a wall, left knee bent, and right leg straight and extended back (see figure 7.3).

2. Press the right heel into the floor.

3. Repeat with the left leg back.

Figure 7.3   Standing calf stretch.

Standing Hamstrings Stretch

1. Stand with the left leg forward, right knee slightly bent.

2. Bend at the waist and reach both arms toward the left toe, while simultaneously bending the left toe toward the fingers (see figure 7.4).

3. Repeat on the other leg.

Figure 7.4   Standing hamstrings stretch.

Torso Stretch

1. Stand with your feet shoulder-width apart and hands on your hips.
2. Slowly rotate your torso in circular motion to the front, left, back, and right (see figure 7.5).
3. Repeat.

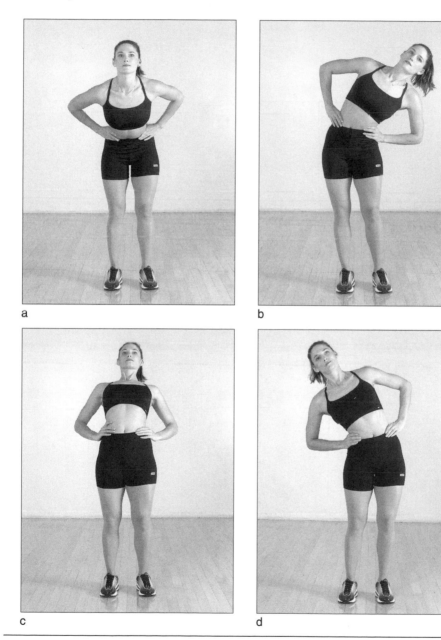

Figure 7.5 Torso stretch.

Achilles Stretch

1. Stand with one leg slightly in front of the other.
2. Bend both knees slightly to stretch the calf (see figure 7.6).
3. Repeat with the other leg forward.

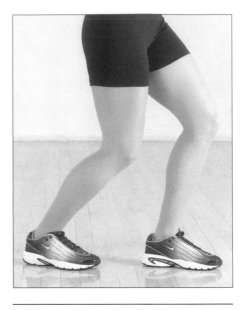

Figure 7.6 Achilles stretch.

Hip Adductor Stretch

1. Position yourself with your left knee bent and left foot slightly toward the left; extend the right leg back with the right foot parallel with the left foot. Extend arms and place hands even with the left foot (see figure 7.7).
2. Push forward with your left leg, but don't allow the knee to go over the toe.
3. Repeat with the right leg forward.

Figure 7.7 Hip adductor stretch.

Jump Rope Warm-Up Programs

The basic, intermediate, and advanced warm-up programs that follow should be performed at 60 to 80 percent of the MHR.

The 15 jumping techniques are designed to simulate a wide range of athletic movements. Try to incorporate all of them for a total-body warm-up.

One reason rope jumping is an extremely effective training activity is that an athlete can use it to enhance a wide range of athletic capacities in one session. The 15 jumping techniques, even in a warm-up, can cultivate balance, rhythm, timing, agility, coordination, quickness, speed, and power.

BASIC WARM-UP PROGRAM

Bounce step

Alternate-foot step

Side straddle

Forward straddle

Skier's jump

Bell jump

All seasons

Use the standard measurement in the beginning. In order to correctly measure results, wait one week before possibly shortening the rope to execute faster turns or increasing the intensity level.

Bounce step, alternate-foot step, side straddle, forward straddle, skier's jump, bell jump

Training routine	1. 4 reps of bounce step 2. 4 reps of alternate-foot step 3. Repeat for 2.5 minutes 4. 4 reps each of side straddle, forward straddle, skier's jump, bell jump 5. Repeat for 2.5 minutes
Duration	5 minutes
Intensity	60-65% of MHR or 120-130 RPM
Goal	Move forward, backward, and laterally while jumping

INTERMEDIATE WARM-UP PROGRAM

Bounce step   Alter

Side straddle   Forward straddle

Skier's jump   Bell jump

X-foot cross

Full twister

Arm crossover

Side swing to power jump

All seasons

ROPE MEASUREMENT

Use the standard measurement. In order to correctly measure results, wait one week before possibly adjusting the length of the rope.

TECHNIQUES

Bounce step, alternate-foot step, side straddle, forward straddle, skier's jump, bell jump, X-foot cross, full twister, arm crossover, side swing to power jump

Training routine	1. Perform 8 reps of each technique 2. Repeat for a total of 5 minutes
Duration	5 minutes
Intensity	65-70% of MHR or 130-140 RPM
Goal	Move forward, backward, and laterally while jumping

ADVANCED WARM-UP PROGRAM

Bounce step   Alternate-foot step   High step

Side straddle   Forward straddle

Skier's jump   Bell jump

Full twister   X-foot cross

Forward shuffle   Backward shuffle   Heel to toe

Backward jumping   Arm crossover

Side swing to jump   Power jump

All seasons

Use the chest measurement. Wait one week before possibly shortening the rope.

Bounce step, alternate-foot step, high step, side straddle, forward straddle, skier's jump, bell jump, full twister, X-foot cross, forward shuffle, backward shuffle, heel to toe, backward jumping, arm crossover, side swing to jump, power jump

Training routine	1. Perform 12 reps of each technique 2. Repeat for a total of 5 minutes
Duration	5 minutes
Intensity	70-80% of MHR or 140-180 RPM
Goal	Move forward, backward, and laterally while jumping Gradually increase intensity

How Michael Gostigian, Three-Time Olympic Pentathlete, Made the Jump Rope His Best Friend

"Rope jumping is the most underrated exercise there is," says Michael Gostigian. "Not a day goes by that I don't use your jump rope and system. In every practice I use it for warming up in fencing, weight training, and even for swimming. I need it! A 5- to 10-minute session on the pool deck saves me from spending excessive time and mental energy in the water. Also, I use it as a substitute for my running when there is inclement weather.

"As you know, your jump rope and system is an athlete's best training partner. So thanks for helping me out and being an integral part of my Olympic training."

CHAPTER

8

GAIN SPEED AND QUICKNESS

Quickness and speed of the hands and feet are two athletic attributes that directly contribute to competitive advantages in most sports. Rope jumping is a training tool that enhances this quickness and speed without requiring large blocks of training time or numerous sessions a week.

My sprint training programs can generate dramatic quickness of the hands and feet because of the sheer number of executions that must take place in a short period of time. Performing 100 jumps in 30 seconds forces the wrists to turn in excess of three times a second! The feet must move at the same frequency and the goal is to make contact with the surface as short as possible. For athletes who can jump 120 times or more in 30 seconds, this translates not only into the wrists turning four times a second, but the feet executing four touches a second!

Hand and foot speeds of 3-5 times per second at 30- to 120-second durations train targeted fast-twitch muscle fibers in the upper and lower body to gradually function at norms approaching these high levels of execution. In other words, athletes will discover that they are able to operate more comfortably in high-speed or extremely rapid sports conditions, which will result in improved performance and effectiveness. Many sports don't require anaerobic bursts of up to two minutes. For athletes in these sports, shorter durations are sufficient.

Billy Stearns, who coaches many of the top junior tennis players in the country, incorporated my jump rope training system into his program and noticed significant improvement in his players in just four weeks.

Jorg Rauthe, women's tennis coach at Manhattanville College, said that Stearns's players "moved like cats across the court" during a visit that took place after Stearns initiated my jump rope training system. Upon his return to New York, Coach Rauthe recommended that the school's athletic director introduce all athletes and school sports programs to this system. Coach Rauthe was already a believer in jump rope training, but he became more educated after participating in my clinic for the Tennis Teacher's Conference at the U.S. Tennis Open. He now realizes that tennis players and other athletes benefit most from *sport-specific* jump rope training programs.

Also, because the feet are rising just high enough from the surface to clear the rope, athletes will become "light on the feet." This is a term that refers to a graceful athletic ability to not only move quickly, but rapidly change direction or speed.

Athletes in sports requiring these types of movements move in a distinct way. They often scamper across the playing surface, *barely lifting their feet from the surface.* This is especially true when they are changing directions or speeds. Their feet look as if they are gliding along the surface.

This is the main reason why my programs demand that athletes lift the feet just high enough to execute proper jump rope movements. It simulates what actually takes place while they move in sports competitions.

The sprint training programs will also strengthen muscle groups in the upper and lower body. That's because fast-twitch muscle fibers are generally those muscle fibers targeted in other sprint training exercises.

Over a 4- to 6-week period, after the execution of any of the four levels, athletes will do the following:

- Dramatically strengthen the wrists and forearms and noticeably improve grip strength, something especially important to athletes in racket sports and to hitters in baseball
- Develop powerful calves and quadriceps
- Develop shoulder and back muscles
- Greatly improve posture and balance

Another benefit of the sprint training programs is that they generate and simulate the concentration intensity demanded of high-level sports competition. So, in addition to the physical training benefits, athletes

Tennis requires players to be light on their feet, an attribute that can be developed through movement simulation in rope jumping.

will gain mental focusing skills necessary for controlled, maximum exertion—the mental edge that often determines who wins or loses.

Preparing for the Sprint Programs

My sprint training programs are ideal quickness and speed-building programs. They are the first programs that use a baseline to measure improvements in proficiency and conditioning (as discussed in chapter 6, page 69).

However, these programs should be executed only after athletes have mastered basic rope jumping skills and established a jump rope capacity and a training baseline of *at least 100 jumps in 30 seconds or 200 jumps in 60 seconds* using the alternate-foot step. The alternate-foot step is the technique that will be used during the sprint training programs. Remember to count the right foot only and multiply by 2 to get the total count for each set. I also recommend that athletes reestablish their training baseline each week for the timed sprint programs. Depending on the duration of the sets in the program, use a 30-, 60-, 90-, or 120-second pretest. As jump rope proficiency and endurance improve, so will your baseline score.

Tables 8.1 and 8.2 give two examples of pretests, using 30 seconds and 60 seconds, respectively. These are explained more fully in chapter 6 (page 70).

Athletes should use the offseason to master jump rope skills and establish a jump rope capacity and a training baseline. The athletes should then use the preseason to complete the levels of the sprint training program that best meet the demands of their sport. During the in-season, athletes should train often enough to improve and maintain the conditioning and athletic capacities developed during the preseason.

Table 8.1 Pretest Example 1: 30 Seconds

Time Jump 3 times	Reps for alternate-foot step Record the reps for each set (count right foot, multiply by 2)	Baseline score Add reps of all sets and divide by 3
30 sec	50 jumps × 2 = 100	
30 sec	52 jumps × 2 = 104	306 jumps / 3 = 102 (baseline)
30 sec	51 jumps × 2 = 102	

Table 8.2 Pretest Example 2: 60 Seconds

Time Jump 3 times	Reps for alternate-foot step Record the reps for each set (count right foot, multiply by 2)	Baseline score Add reps of all sets and divide by 3
60 sec	100 jumps × 2 = 200	
60 sec	104 jumps × 2 = 208	612 jumps / 3 = 204 (baseline)
60 sec	102 jumps × 2 = 204	

Sprint Programs

On the next pages are the following sprint programs: basic and intermediate programs, and basic, intermediate, and advanced timed sprint programs. The timed programs require the athlete to first have a well-trained aerobic base to maintain intensity and lessen recovery time. Be sure to do a more specific warm-up before and cool-down after each jump session to lower the risk of injury.

Perform the presprint conditioning programs during the first two weeks before attempting the timed basic, intermediate, and advanced programs. Each sprint program session should last between 5 and 10 minutes. This is plenty of time to create appropriate anaerobic stress levels to trigger noticeable training effects.

Establish 24-hour rest periods between sessions to allow the body to adequately recover from the stress of high-intensity rope jumping. Again, because the body is pushed to the edge of its anaerobic threshold ($\dot{V}O_2$max), the recovery strategy from high-intensity jump rope training should mimic that of other high-intensity sprint training programs.

The ratio between jumping and resting for the basic program should start at 1 to 1 (for example, jump 30 seconds and rest 30 seconds). As your anaerobic conditioning level improves and your recovery time decreases, jump and rest at a 2-to-1 ratio (for example, jump 30 seconds and rest 15 seconds).

The intermediate program extends the jump rope durations to 60 seconds a set, followed by a 60-second rest period. There should be five sets a session. Athletes should do three sessions a week during the preseason. As noted earlier, allow for 24-hour rest periods between sessions. Use a 60-second pretest to establish a baseline.

The first advanced program extends jump rope durations to 90 seconds a set, with a 60-second rest period, in five sets a session. Again, most athletes will find three sets a week in the preseason adequate to create noticeable training benefits. The proportionally reduced resting period is established to put greater stress on the anaerobic energy system. This also approximates the timeout breaks of many sports. Use a 90-second pretest to establish a baseline.

The second advanced program extends jump rope durations to 120 seconds a set, with a 60-second rest period between sets in five sets a session. Boxers and highly conditioned athletes who use anaerobic power for longer durations can choose this level to really push the envelope. For most athletes, five sets of 120-second anaerobic bursts should be enough to reach the highest level of anaerobic fitness. Use a 120-second pretest to establish a baseline.

BASIC PRESPRINT CONDITIONING PROGRAM

Alternate-foot step

SEASON

Off-season and preseason

ROPE MEASUREMENT

Use the standard measurement in the beginning. In order to correctly measure results, wait one week before possibly shortening the rope.

TECHNIQUE

Alternate-foot step

Training routine	1. 50 reps of alternate-foot step followed by 30-second rest 2. Repeat 3 times 3. 75 reps of alternate-foot step followed by 45-second rest 4. Repeat 2 times 5. 100 reps of alternate-foot step followed by 60-second rest
Intensity	Jump at 85-90% of MHR or 180-200 RPM
Goal	Each set should equal or increase baseline score

INTERMEDIATE PRESPRINT CONDITIONING PROGRAM

Alternate-foot step

Off-season and preseason

ROPE MEASUREMENT

Use the standard measurement in the beginning. In order to correctly measure results, wait one week before possibly shortening the rope.

TECHNIQUE

Alternate-foot step

Training routine	1. 100 reps of alternate-foot step followed by 60-second rest 2. Repeat 3 times 3. 75 reps of alternate-foot step followed by 45-second rest 4. Repeat 4 times 5. 50 reps of alternate-foot step followed by 30-second rest 6. Repeat 2 times
Intensity	Jump at 85-90% of MHR or 180-200 RPM
Goal	Each set should increase intensity

BASIC SPRINT PROGRAM

Alternate-foot step

Preseason and in-season

ROPE MEASUREMENT

Use the standard or chest measurement in the beginning. In order to correctly measure results, wait one week before possibly shortening the rope.

TECHNIQUE

Alternate-foot step

Training routine	1. Perform alternate-foot step for a total of 30 seconds 2. Rest 30 seconds 3. Repeat 5 times
Duration	5 minutes: 2.5 minutes jump time, 2.5 minutes rest time
Intensity	Jump at 85-95% of MHR (180-220 RPM) with 10-second bursts at 95+% of MHR (220+ RPM)
Goal	Each set should equal or increase baseline score and decrease the rest periods between sets

INTERMEDIATE SPRINT PROGRAM

Alternate-foot step

SEASON

Preseason and in-season

ROPE MEASUREMENT

Use the chest or lower rib cage measurement. In order to correctly measure results, wait one week before possibly shortening the rope.

TECHNIQUE

Alternate-foot step

Training routine	1. Perform alternate-foot step for a total of 60 seconds 2. Rest 60 seconds 3. Repeat 5 times
Duration	10 minutes: 5 minutes jump time, 5 minutes rest time
Intensity	Jump at 85-95% of MHR (180-220 RPM) with 10-second bursts at 95+% of MHR (220+ RPM)
Goal	Each set should equal or increase baseline score and decrease the rest periods between sets

ADVANCED SPRINT PROGRAM I

Alternate-foot step

Preseason and in-season

ROPE MEASUREMENT

Use the lower rib cage measurement.

TECHNIQUE

Alternate-foot step

Training routine	1. Perform alternate-foot step for a total of 90 seconds 2. Rest 60 seconds 3. Repeat 5 times
Duration	12.5 minutes: 7.5 minutes jump time, 5 minutes rest time
Intensity	Jump at 85-95% of MHR (180-220 RPM) with 10-second bursts at 95+% of MHR (220+ RPM)
Goal	Each set should equal or increase baseline score and decrease the rest periods between sets

ADVANCED SPRINT PROGRAM 2

Alternate-foot step

SEASON

Preseason and in-season

ROPE MEASUREMENT

Use the lower rib cage measurement.

TECHNIQUE

Alternate-foot step

Training routine	1. Perform alternate-foot step for a total of 120 seconds 2. Rest 60 seconds 3. Repeat 5 times
Duration	15 minutes: 10 minutes jump time, 5 minutes rest time
Intensity	Jump at 85-95% of MHR (180-220 RPM) with 10-second bursts at 95+% of MHR (220+ RPM)
Goal	Each set should equal or increase baseline score and decrease the rest periods between sets

How the U.S. National Badminton Team Used Rope Jumping to Improve Speed and Quickness

My sprint programs benefit athletes of many sports, including badminton. As an assistant coach for the U.S. national badminton team and a former Indonesian national badminton team member, Ignatius Rusli used rope jumping as a training strategy. He used it as required anaerobic training but knew only the basics. The common workout used was restricted to single, double, triple, and quadruple jumps.

Since I demonstrated my system (using my speed rope), his jump rope program has been far more effective and produced advanced benefits when compared to his former program.

"I strongly recommend that everyone use Buddy Lee's jump rope programs to supplement any workout program. It will benefit anaerobic training as well as explosiveness and quickness," he said.

Kevin Han, three-time Olympian and national badminton champion, adds, "I think especially for our sport, this jump rope system has helped us tremendously in increasing our speed on the court (foot speed, arm speed, and wrist speed, for example). It also has helped us build our endurance and stamina in the long run."

"For badminton, cross-training is the only activity that encompasses all the elements necessary to attain top physical conditioning. Finesse, agility, speed, endurance, quickness, power, and explosiveness have all improved with the use of Buddy's programs," said Erica Von Heiland, a member of the 1992 and 1996 U.S. Olympic badminton teams.

CHAPTER

9

DEVELOP AGILITY, COORDINATION, AND BALANCE

"The body becomes all eyes" is a way to describe an optimal state of awareness that is similar to that of an animal that is ready to respond to any stimuli in its environment.

This is an apt metaphor for adept displays of agility demonstrated by gymnasts, martial artists, basketball players, football players, wrestlers, and athletes performing in sports requiring the complex coordination of multiple muscle groups during the execution of precise movements.

Agility is having full control of the feet and the ability to decelerate, accelerate, and quickly change direction without decreasing speed. Agility also enables athletes to regulate shifts in the body's center of gravity while changing direction.

Most sports require simultaneous movements in several planes. Because sports are generally games of multidirectional movement, agility training is essential. Agility, like speed and other attributes of raw athletic talent, is to some degree genetically determined. It almost seems as if training for it is moot. However, an analysis of agility will reveal ways of developing it as a personal or athletic attribute.

Multiple muscle groups and omnidirectional movements are used in wrestling, so agility training is essential.

Agility is a demonstration of proprioception at its best. It's the proprioceptive capacity of the body that provides a "knowledge" of itself as it moves in three-dimensional space. The challenge for the athlete, then, is to practice activities that develop this sense. It is largely intuitive, but every athlete must cultivate it.

In the past, athletes and their trainers have tried several ways to enhance this sense. Some offensive linemen in football, for example, have taken ballet and dance lessons. There is a lesson here that applies to rope jumping because a key element in dance training is rhythmics.

Developing Rhythm

Rhythmics are large-muscle activities that are performed in time to a regular beat or rhythm. Rhythmic training (movements to a constant beat) is critical to coordinating these large-muscle activities into graceful and efficient athletic or artistic movements.

As an athlete's jump rope proficiency increases, so will the ability to sustain longer periods of jumping. At this point, one need not be extremely conscious of each movement and every muscle group while jumping; rather, one must tune in to the rhythm of jumping itself. This is also how to know one is training at the proper intensity level.

A jump rope rhythm can function like a metronome that synchronizes all the different muscles, muscle groups, and vertical and horizontal forces. This rhythm can become a feeling that is a pure experience of synchronized kinesthetic mechanics. Without knowing it, just by tuning in to this rhythm, athletes are tuning in to their sense of balance, a critical component of agility.

Jumping to a beat or rhythm makes rope jumping an ideal tool for cultivating coordination and agility.

As athletes explore this feeling of rhythm, they'll discover that their ability to refine their rope jumping skill is limited only by their commitment and imagination. Meanwhile, they'll be developing the *sense of awareness* that will result in increased agility and coordination in their sports performance.

It's this sense of rhythm that allows many athletes to turn or stop on a dime. There is something almost magical about this sense because, practically speaking, it seems to be the body's ability to respond as a whole to every demand for movement. In a subtle way this sense of rhythm is a sense of the whole body.

The body is synergistic, so one of the secrets to high performance is multijoint training. For example, one research study compared the muscles and motor control systems of concert pianists, elite Olympic swimmers, and weightlifters with those of normal healthy adults. The investigators concluded that it was in *orchestrating the work of several muscles, not in the control of individual muscles,* that the elite performers excelled.

Increasing Kinesthetic Awareness

There's another reason why rope jumping is a powerful agility training tool. In addition to providing a metronome-like rhythm to synchronize the movements of multiple muscle groups, it enhances *neuromuscular coordination* in another very important way. To best understand how this additional training benefit works, let's briefly review the rope jumping experience.

Rope jumping as a training activity draws on nearly every muscle in the body. As athletes increase in proficiency and are able to sustain rope jumping for as long as 5 minutes at a time, they experience how each muscle group, in subtle ways, becomes more involved in the exercise.

In the beginning, it will seem as if it's primarily an exercise of the legs and arms. However, as training continues, athletes will notice that they are making subtle adjustments in posture to ensure they're getting the most out of each jump and swing of the rope. This may include keeping the body erect and the head squarely on the shoulders while focusing straight ahead.

This effort will be accompanied by several adjustments the body will make on its own that will result in increased efficiency of movement and use of energy. This natural kinesthetic and proprioceptive adaptation will develop not only agility and coordination, but also increase the sense of balance and rhythm.

As training continues, athletes will become more aware of how often they're applying the *monitoring* attention style on a regular basis. Rope jumping, no matter how proficient you become, requires you to constantly monitor your execution, even if this monitoring has been focused on the rhythm of the exercise.

It's the monitoring of this experience that is critical to developing the kinesthetic and proprioceptive senses that are critical to agility. Just the act of monitoring is enough to get the body to make numerous corrective neuromuscular adjustments that will lead to sustaining increasingly longer periods of continuation (durations of jumping between catches of the rope).

Even missteps and catches of the rope further develop the kinesthetic and proprioceptive senses, enhancing agility, balance, and coordination. For example, if the body loses the rope, it must recover its balance with each pass of the rope. It must do this while it is synchronizing the centripetal and centrifugal forces of swinging the rope with each jump. Because of the ever-present possibility of missteps during rope jumping sessions, the jumper's attention expands to encompass all aspects of the activity, which includes the whole body. An increased ability to recover from missteps and continue jumping, especially during complex routines, further enhances balance, coordination, and agility.

Managing this process requires the application of the monitoring attention style that allows the body to make the subtle neuromuscular adjustments to sustain progressively longer periods of continuation. These capabilities will manifest themselves in increased sports performance while cultivating an increased sense of grace and fluidity in the athlete's everyday movements. The constant effort to synchronize and coordinate multiple muscle groups in rhythmic patterns in itself develops a sense of grace and a greater sense of comfort with one's own body.

The primary effect of agility training is increased body control resulting from a concentrated form of kinesthetic awareness. Athletes who incorporate effective, consistent agility programs into their training often talk of stunning gains in athleticism, no matter what the sport.

Rope jumping as an agility training tool helps the "body become all eyes" by enhancing proprioceptive senses while maximizing the athlete's kinesthetic awareness. Increased efficiency also manifests itself as improvements in balance, timing, and rhythm.

Circuit Training Program

This program should be executed only after athletes have mastered basic rope jumping skills and established a jump rope capacity and a training baseline of *at least 100 jumps in 30 seconds* using the alternate-foot step (counting the right foot and multiplying by 2 to get the number of total jumps in the set) and *at least 30 power jumps in 30 seconds*. I also recommend that athletes reestablish their training baseline each week. It can take several years to reach your maximum baseline, therefore you can keep jumping to attain an even higher level of fitness. So as jump rope proficiency, endurance, and intensity improve, so will your baseline score.

Tables 9.1 and 9.2 give examples of the pretest that establishes a training baseline for the circuit training program, using the alternate-foot step and basic power jump.

Table 9.1   Pretest Example 1: 30 Seconds

Time Jump 3 times	Reps for alternate-foot step Record the reps for each set (count right foot, multiply by 2)	Baseline score Add reps of all sets and divide by 3
30 sec	50 jumps $\times$ 2 = 100	
30 sec	52 jumps $\times$ 2 = 104	306 jumps / 3 = 102 (baseline)
30 sec	51 jumps $\times$ 2 = 102	

Table 9.2   Pretest Example 2: 60 Seconds

Time Jump 3 times	Reps for power jump Record the reps for each set	Baseline score Add reps of all sets and divide by 3
60 sec	100 jumps $\times$ 2 = 200	
60 sec	104 jumps $\times$ 2 = 208	612 jumps / 3 = 204 (baseline)
60 sec	102 jumps $\times$ 2 = 204	

ADVANCED CIRCUIT TRAINING PROGRAM

1. SPEED STATION

Alternate-foot step

2. POWER STATION

Power jump

3. FINESSE STATION

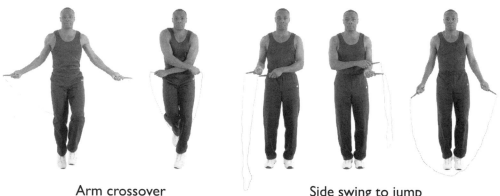

Arm crossover   Side swing to jump

SEASON

In-season

ROPE MEASUREMENT

Use the standard measurement in the beginning. In order to correctly measure results, wait one week before possibly shortening the rope.

TECHNIQUES

All techniques in chapter 3

Training routine	Phase 1: Perform all sports cross-training jumps in chapter 3 for a total of 6 minutes at 75-80% of MHR or 160-180 RPM
	Phase 2: Rotate between the circuit stations 4 times for a total of 4 minutes
Circuit stations	Speed jumping, power jumping, finesse jumping
Station 1: **Speed jumping** **Alternate-foot step**	Jump 30 seconds, active rest 30 seconds (jog in place)
Station 2: **Power jumping** **Power jump**	Jump 30 seconds, active rest 30 seconds (jog in place)
Station 3: **Finesse Jumping** **Arm crossover** **Side swing to jump**	Jump 30 seconds, active rest 30 seconds (jog in place)
Duration	10 minutes: 8 minutes jump time, 2 minutes rest time
Intensity for stations	85-95+% of MHR or 180-220+ RPM
Goal	To decrease the active rest periods between each station

How One World Champion Used Rope Jumping to Improve Agility and Coordination

Audrey Weisiger, two-time U.S. Olympic coach and former coach of Michael Weiss, two-time Olympian and World bronze medalist, uses rope jumping as part of the training and conditioning program for all of her young athletes. She is particularly impressed with how rope jumping has increased the efficiency of movement of her athletes.

Efficient movements allow athletes to conserve energy while executing complex movements on the one hand and to employ energy strategically on the other. By streamlining energy expenditure, efficiency of movement leads to *increases in endurance and stamina.*

Weisiger adds that rope jumping not only teaches her athletes how to jump properly, which prevents injury, it also teaches them to jump while keeping their torsos upright, a critical requirement to jumping with ice skates.

Justin Pekarek, 1999 world ice dance champion, says, "When I combined your Hyperformance speed rope with the many skills and jumps you showed me, my agility went through the roof. I have found training with your rope and program interesting, challenging, and, most of all, fun."

CHAPTER 10

BOOST STRENGTH AND POWER

Sports such as volleyball, basketball, skating, soccer, track and field, and wrestling require bursts of energy (power and explosiveness) at decisive moments to execute critical movements. The vertical jump test is one way to measure power and explosiveness. Stand in the universal athletic position (see chapter 1, page 2) and jump up as high as you can to touch a mark on the wall. Although vertical leap is largely determined by genetics, training techniques such as weight training, jumping rope, and plyometrics exercises can increase the explosive power and height of each jump.

How Rope Jumping Increases Power and Explosiveness

Explosiveness is generated by forceful contractions of fast-twitch muscle fibers that can generate and sustain speed. It can be described as force plus quickness. My power jump rope training programs will show how to generate and project explosiveness into critical movements of different sports.

For example, a high vertical jump has its merits, but a competitive edge normally comes from advantages in vertical acceleration: how quickly athletes jump from a standing position or how fast they react from a position of readiness. My power jump rope programs reduce the gap between the height of the jump and the subsequent takeoff phase by minimizing surface contact time.

Rope jumping has often been referred to as an effective warm-up to plyometrics exercises, but it is itself a low-intensity plyometrics exercise that produces significant training benefits that can trigger superior athletic performance.

Combining rope jumping with strengthening exercises during the season's training cycles can significantly improve explosiveness and power in sports performance. That's because rope jumping is an exercise that forces the neuromuscular system to respond more quickly and forcefully.

Plyometrics exercises can be traced back to the former Eastern bloc countries. Over the past years, more American coaches and athletes

Soccer players need bursts of energy for kicking, running, and quickly changing direction.

have learned how to use these exercises to improve overall athletic performance. Still, many coaches have little experience in how to effectively implement a seasonal plyometrics program for athletes of different ages, levels, and abilities. Rope jumping, on the other hand, is very effective and safe for both young and mature athletes, because jumps can be repeated hundreds of times in one session without risk of injury.

Plyometrics is designed not only to increase speed and explosiveness but also jumping ability. The principle is simple: The more a muscle is stretched, the more powerful its subsequent contraction. The goal of plyometrics is to shorten the interval between a stretched muscle and its contraction.

Plyometrics uses gravity to force the stretching of a muscle while the athlete propels in the opposite direction to train the muscle to contract with power. For example, stepping or leaping off a raised surface will force the leg muscles to stretch as the knees bend to absorb the impact of the landing. The athlete then contracts the quadriceps and hamstrings in a burst of propulsion during a leap or step forward. It's the stretching of the muscle that stores the energy for the subsequent explosive takeoff phase. This is how repeated plyometrics training builds explosive power in the legs.

The same principle is at work in jump rope training. Energy is stored in the legs on the landing phase of each jump and is released on each successive jump. Unlike most other plyometrics exercises, rope jumping allows this activity to be repeated hundreds of times per session. Because of the number of repetitions and the various levels of intensity possible during each rope jumping session, it can also produce aerobic and anaerobic training effects. This is the principle at work in my jump rope training system.

This system's emphasis on repeated jumps also underscores a plyometrics principle that emphasizes the force production of *eccentric* (stretched) contractions over *concentric* (shortened) contractions. In jumping rope, the concentric contraction takes place during the landing phase of each jump. This landing phase progresses into the subsequent takeoff phase (eccentric) contraction of each jump. The gravity-assisted landing phase (concentric) contraction provides the force necessary for the explosiveness executed on each subsequent jump. By jumping less than an inch from the surface and landing lightly on the balls of the feet, the neuromuscular

*T*his system further reduces the stretch-shortening cycle by emphasizing repeated and quick jumps, which trains the athlete to reach maximum vertical and horizontal acceleration in the shortest period of time.

system becomes thoroughly trained in and adapts to this key principle of plyometrics.

High-speed eccentric contractions draw on fast-twitch muscle fibers while also producing more force per motor unit. This neuromuscular process explains how jump rope training produces a reduced stretch-shortening cycle that allows the athlete to derive the greatest benefits from a plyometrics program.

As the athlete develops greater rope jumping proficiency, the reduced gap between eccentric and concentric contractions offers a greater potential for improved athletic performance. For example, rope jumping will enhance an athlete's capacity to rapidly execute successive jumps or extended sequences of vertical acceleration while also improving reaction time.

Power Programs

I have developed five power jump rope training programs that emphasize improving anaerobic capacity, vertical acceleration, grip strength, and start speed. In addition, they provide the following benefits:

- Increased wrist, ankle, and knee strength
- Conditioning of the back, shoulders, and chest
- Improved posture
- Increased proprioception of the feet and ankles
- Increased strength in the calves, quadriceps, and hamstrings
- Improvements in vertical leap and lateral shifting

These programs should be executed only after athletes have mastered the basic rope jumping skills and established a jump rope capacity and a training baseline of *at least 30 power jumps in 30 seconds or 60 power jumps in 60 seconds.* Athletes should reestablish their training baseline each week. Baselines can be set in 30- or 60-second pretests. As jump rope proficiency and endurance improve, so will your baseline score.

Tables 10.1 and 10.2 give examples of the pretest to use for establishing a training baseline for the power programs. The basic power jump (two rope revolutions per jump) is the technique that will be used for all power training programs, so it is also used for the pretest.

Table 10.1 Pretest Example 1: 30 Seconds

Time Sprint 3 sets	Reps for power jump Record the reps for each set	Baseline score Add reps of all sets and divide by 3
30 sec	40 jumps	126 jumps / 3 = 42 (baseline)
30 sec	45 jumps	
30 sec	41 jumps	

Table 10.2 Pretest Example 2: 60 Seconds

Time Sprint 3 sets	Reps for power jump Record the reps for each set	Baseline score Add reps of all sets and divide by 3
60 sec	80 jumps	252 jumps / 3 = 84 (baseline)
60 sec	90 jumps	
60 sec	82 jumps	

BASIC PRECONDITIONING POWER PROGRAM

Alternate-foot step

Power jump

SEASON

Off-season and preseason

ROPE MEASUREMENT

Use the standard measurement in the beginning. In order to correctly measure results, wait one week before possibly shortening the rope.

TECHNIQUES

Alternate-foot step, power jump

Training routine	1. 8 reps of alternate-foot step 2. 4 reps of consecutive power jumps 3. Repeat this routine for 30 seconds 4. Rest for 30 seconds 5. Repeat 5 times
Duration	5 minutes: 2.5 minutes jump time, 2.5 minutes rest time
Intensity	Jump at 85-90% of MHR
Goal	Maintain the same speed from the alternate-foot step to the power jump Decrease the rest periods between sets

INTERMEDIATE PRECONDITIONING POWER PROGRAM

Alternate-foot step

Power jump

Off-season and preseason

ROPE MEASUREMENT

Use the standard measurement in the beginning. In order to correctly measure results, wait one week before possibly shortening the rope.

TECHNIQUES

Alternate-foot step, power jump

Training routine	1. 8 reps of alternate-foot step (count right foot 4 times) 2. 8 reps of consecutive power jumps 3. Repeat this routine for 60 seconds 4. Rest for 60 seconds 5. Repeat 3 times
Duration	6 minutes: 3 minutes jump time, 3 minutes rest time
Intensity	Jump at 85-90% of MHR
Goal	Maintain same speed from alternate-foot step to power jump Decrease the rest periods between sets

BASIC POWER PROGRAM

Power jump

SEASON

Off-season and preseason

ROPE MEASUREMENT

Use the standard measurement. In order to correctly measure results, wait one week before possibly shortening the rope.

TECHNIQUE

Power jump

Training routine	1. Power jump 30 seconds 2. Rest 30 seconds 3. Repeat 5 times
Duration	5 minutes: 2.5 minutes jump time, 2.5 minutes rest time
Intensity	Jump at 85-95% of MHR or 80-120 RPM power
Goal	Move forward and backward while jumping Decrease the rest periods between sets

INTERMEDIATE POWER PROGRAM

Power jump

SEASON

Preseason and in-season

ROPE MEASUREMENT

Use the chest measurement. In order to correctly measure results, wait one week before possibly shortening the rope.

TECHNIQUE

Power jump

Training routine	1. Power jump 60 seconds 2. Rest 60 seconds 3. Repeat 5 times
Duration	10 minutes: 5 minutes jump time, 5 minutes rest time
Intensity	Jump at 85-95% of MHR or 80-120 RPM power
Goal	Move forward and backward while jumping Decrease the rest periods between sets

ADVANCED POWER PROGRAM I

Power jump   Side straddle

Forward straddle

SEASON

Preseason and in-season

ROPE MEASUREMENT

Use the chest measurement. In order to correctly measure results, wait one week before possibly shortening the rope.

TECHNIQUES

Power jump, power side straddle, power forward straddle

Training routine	1. Perform 2 reps of each technique
	2. Repeat this routine for 30 seconds
	3. Rest 30 seconds
	4. Repeat 5 times
Duration	5 minutes: 2.5 minutes jump time, 2.5 minutes rest time
Intensity	Jump at 85-95% of MHR
Goal	Move forward and backward while jumping
	Decrease the rest periods between sets

Power jump

Skier's jump

Bell jump

Full twister

X-foot cross

Forward straddle

Side straddle   Arm crossover

Preseason and in-season

ROPE MEASUREMENT

Use the chest to lower ribcage measurement. In order to correctly measure results, wait one week before possibly shortening the rope.

TECHNIQUES

Power jump, power skier's jump, power bell jump, power twister, power X-foot cross, power forward straddle, power side straddle, power arm crossover

Training repetitions	1. Perform 2 reps of each technique 2. Repeat this routine for 30 seconds 3. Rest 30 seconds 4. Repeat 5 times
Duration	5 minutes: 2.5 minutes jump time, 2.5 minutes rest time
Intensity	Jump at 85-95% of MHR
Goal	Decrease the rest periods between sets

How Kurt Angle, Olympic Gold Medal Wrestler, Used Rope Jumping to Develop Explosiveness and Power

In 1996, I helped cross-train several athletes from different sports while also competing for a spot on the 1996 U. S. Olympic Greco-Roman wrestling team at the U.S. Olympic Training Center in Colorado Springs, Colorado. That's when I met Kurt Angle in the USOC's strength and conditioning room, where we lifted weights, did plyometrics, and jumped rope.

At the time, he was jumping with a segmented beaded rope that was turning very slowly. I asked Kurt why he was jumping with such a slow rope.

He said, "Man, Buddy, your rope is too fast for me."

I said, "What do you mean by 'too fast'?"

Kurt was another world-class athlete working hard to maintain the winning edge. They say the struggle of staying on top is as tough as getting there. Kurt was ranked number one in the country and was the reigning world champion at 220 pounds. He had an incredible physique and was in great condition but was missing the key that could make the winning difference.

I looked at Kurt and asked, "How do you wrestle on the mat? Do you wrestle slowly or with speed and power?"

Kurt answered, "With speed and power."

I told him that in order to get the maximum benefits from jumping rope for wrestling, he had to train with the rope in the way he wanted to perform in his sport. In other words, he had to train at the same intensity with which he competed. He immediately understood because he was looking for an edge to win in a very tough weight class with two world champions going for the gold— Kurt and the former world champion from Iran. Wrestling is the national sport in Iran and the country is known for producing many of the world's greatest wrestling legends.

That same day, I showed Kurt how to jump with my speed rope because he had already mastered the basic jump rope skills. I demonstrated a few basic foot movements combined with the power jump. After a little while Kurt was not only training at a higher intensity, he was having fun and jumping at an explosive level. Kurt Angle "converted" and became a believer in the speed rope. In the 1996 Atlanta Olympic Games he combined quickness, strength, and efficient movements to generate the power and explosiveness that gave him the competitive edge in those final seconds of the gold medal match, winning the medal.

After the Olympics he said, "I train with the Buddy Lee jump rope twice a week. It is phenomenally quick and has helped me to train better than ever. I am more explosive!"

Kurt later invited me to come to his wrestling training camp in Pittsburgh, PA, to show other young wrestlers how to get the maximum training benefits from jumping rope. A couple of years later Kurt went on to television entertainment and is now a professional world wrestling champion, known nationwide as one of the superheroes for the WWE (World Wrestling Entertainment).

CHAPTER

11

CONDITION FOR SPECIFIC SPORTS AND FITNESS GOALS

Rope jumping is considered a total body movement that can apply to almost any sport. In order to maximize the benefits of a jump rope regimen, you should strive to simulate your sport in form, intensity, duration, and sport-specific movements.

Simulation is the key principle for choosing training programs that will quickly help you reach your fitness and sports training goals. Once you have mastered basic rope jumping skills, established sufficient jump rope capacity, and recorded a reliable pretest, you'll be ready for what will be the most challenging part of your training. This step, however, can't be taken unless you've worked through the previous ones.

There are two principles of simulation. First, I designed the programs to draw upon anaerobic energy systems in time intervals that match the energy demands of sports play. For example, a football player relies almost exclusively upon anaerobic energy systems. Each play lasts only for a few seconds, with few plays lasting as long as 10 seconds. The athlete must be able to explode with maximum effort during these intervals. These intervals, however, are normally followed by 45- to 60-second rest periods. Therefore, a football player should modify the jump rope programs in this book to incorporate the intervals into his training thus: 10

Combining simulated sports movements with cycles of simulated energy demands of your sport produces a synergistic effect that willdramaticallyincrease fitness and sports performance.

to 30 seconds of power jumping, followed by 30 seconds of a relaxed bounce step, followed by 10 to 30 more seconds of sprint jumping, for up to five minutes.

Second, I designed programs that are particularly tailored to mimic important movements of sports play. A sprinter's program should emphasize foot speed, balance, and pure anaerobic exertion. A skater's program should focus on agility, balance, and grace. A boxer's program should stress not only footwork but quickness of the hands.

The energy system demands of the sport and its sport-specific movements will define which techniques or combinations of techniques an athlete uses to best simulate his or her sport. Ideally, an athlete's program should simulate that athlete's performance ideal.

Sports requiring explosive movements, sprints, or vertical acceleration should emphasize power jumping techniques. Sports requiring omnidirectional movements during rapidly changing situations should concentrate on agility programs. Sprinters and runners should emphasize the alternate-foot step and high step jumping techniques that simulate running and sprinting for those durations and intensity levels that match their performance ideal.

In addition to these training effects, most athletic movements are part of or are preceded by some form of simulated jumping. This includes the explosive side-to-side movements of a tennis player, the artful dodging of a football running back, the rapid pivots of a basketball player, and the spring of a wrestler. If you examine any athletic movement, you will see a simulation or the activation of a jumping movement.

Rope Jumping During Off-Season, Preseason, and In-Season Training

Knowing how to implement rope jumping during the seasonal training cycles of your sport will make all the difference in receiving the maximum training effects. Usually, a progressive jump rope conditioning program takes around four to six weeks to start producing noticeable improvements in athletic performance.

During the seasonal training cycles rope jumping can be incorporated as a conditioner of the cardiovascular system and a developer of athletic skills and capacities, and it can serve as an efficient warm-up to stretching exercises by increasing circulation to all major muscles.

Off-Season

The off-season is the ideal time to learn how to jump rope and develop a strong aerobic foundation. It is also a time when athletes should recover, repair needs, and gain more knowledge about their sport. During the off-season, learn the basic jump rope skills in chapter 2 and work through the four-step conditioning program in chapters 4 and 5, while incorporating the 15 jump rope training techniques in chapter 3.

Learning to jump in the off-season also reduces the risk of embarrassment that results from feeling awkward in front of teammates. Some athletes in team sports may quickly become discouraged if they are unable to master new techniques in a short time. Mastering basic jump rope principles takes some time, so it's best to tackle it during the time of the year when the athlete has ample time and space to learn and practice at his or her own pace.

Jumping rope in the off-season serves to continue conditioning athletes while improving their athletic abilities during these critical months of development. Athletes should use this time to work on strengths and weaknesses and total body conditioning. Practice rope jumping as often as three to five times a week to develop a 10-minute basic jump rope

---

Off-Season Rope Jumping

During this developmental stage, learn the skill of jumping and work on increasing jump rope capacity.

- Master the skill of jumping (see the preparation phase in the four-step conditioning program in chapter 4).

- Develop a jump rope capacity (see the intermediate and conditioning phase in the four-step conditioning program in chapter 4).

- Increase jump rope intensity (see the sports training phase in the four-step conditioning program in chapter 5).

- Establish a baseline for measuring jump rope intensity (see chapter 6).

- Implement the preconditioning programs.

Frequency: 3 to 5 times per week as a conditioner
Duration: 10 minutes total
Intensity: 70 to 85 percent of the MHR

capacity (see the sports-training phase in chapters 4 and 5), and begin the basic warm-up and preconditioning sprint and power programs. The jump rope conditioning programs should be executed only after athletes have mastered the basic jump rope skills, attained a jump rope capacity, and established a training baseline. In each successive jump rope session, athletes should equal or improve their baseline score (you will find the pretest charts in chapters 6, 8, 9, and 10).

The off-season can also be an excellent time to use rope jumping to lose weight. Jumping at a moderate intensity of 120 to 140 RPM or 60 to 70 percent of the maximum heart rate (MHR) for 30 minutes burns approximately 360 calories per session for a 150-pound person. Combined with proper diet and rest, rope jumping can dramatically help reduce unwanted weight.

Preseason

The greatest benefits of my jump rope training programs will take place during the preseason. During the preseason, athletes' training regimens should simulate their sport in form, content, and intensity so that they are conditioned to handle the physical demands of the sport. Preseason jump rope training also gives the athlete a safe and smooth transition into in-season training. During the preseason, athletes should be prepared to graduate to the basic, intermediate, and advanced jump rope programs. This requires jumping three times a week, which will improve cardiovascular fitness levels for the in-season. Continue to use the warm-up programs daily before sports play.

Preseason Rope Jumping

During the preseason, jump to simulate your sport in form, content, and intensity.

- Establish a new baseline for measuring jump rope intensity.
- Implement the basic through advanced programs.
- Continue to use the warm-up programs.

Frequency: 3 times per week as an aerobic and anaerobic conditioner
Duration: 5 to 10 minutes total
Intensity: 85 to 95 percent of MHR with 10- to 30-second bursts at 95+ percent of MHR

My training programs generate anaerobic stress levels that are similar to those created by weight training or other types of high-intensity resistance training. Rope jumping is a repetitive activity and therefore it's not unusual for athletes to experience lactic acid buildup in the shoulders, forearms, calves, or quadriceps after a session of sprint, agility, or power training. Also, it's quite possible that some athletes may experience delayed muscle soreness after high-intensity jump rope training.

Athletes should do plenty of stretching before, during, and after each jump session to recover properly. Allow for 24 hours of rest between high-intensity and power jump rope training sessions. Ideally, my sprint, power, and circuit training programs should be executed during off-days from resistance training programs.

Athletes will notice significant gains in speed, quickness, agility, explosiveness, and overall conditioning that will supplement their other training programs. They will also have developed an anaerobic fitness level that they'd like to maintain during the in-season.

In-Season

During the in-season, athletes should reach their fitness peak. Athletes can do this by continuing to use the warm-up programs daily before sports play and the advanced training programs 2 to 3 times a week as a conditioner.

Many athletes continue actively training to improve performance areas in their sport well into the in-season, and they can continue my

---

In-Season Rope Jumping

Athletes should have reached their peak aerobic and anaerobic fitness levels and strive for maintenance throughout the in-season.

- Maintain established baseline.
- Continue using the advanced-level programs.
- Continue to use the warm-up programs.

Frequency: 2 to 3 times per week as an anaerobic conditioner; jump daily as warm-up
Duration: 5 minutes total
Intensity: 85 to 95 percent of MHR with 10- to 30-second bursts at 95+ percent of MHR

training programs as well. However, given the wear and tear on the body during competition, the programs should be modified to accommodate critical recovery times from competitive events.

Therefore, athletes should cut back their jump rope training to no more than three sessions a week in the competition phase to allow more recovery time. The goal of in-season training is to maintain sharpened athletic skills and cardiovascular fitness and to improve sports performance. Performing more than three advanced jump rope programs a week can have a negative impact on sports performance by impinging on recovery and other training times.

In the period where athletes compete in the qualifying tournaments for the regionals, states, nationals, and worlds, athletes should only use jump rope as a daily warm-up. Perform the advanced warm-up program during this season. This reduced frequency further accommodates the additional rest required of fatigued bodies as the season winds down.

Sport-Specific Programs

On the following pages you will find specific advice for tailoring a jump rope regimen to your sport or exercise goals. Find your sport on the left side of the table and follow it across for benefits, recommendations, and suggestions for seasonal training. Continue to use the warm-up programs throughout all seasons as discussed in chapter 7.

Program Index

This list contains jump rope programs that are referred to in the following chart of sport-specific regimens and the pages where they can be found.

Four-step conditioning program   58

Basic warm-up program   84
Intermediate warm-up program   86
Advanced warm-up program   88

Basic presprint conditioning program   96
Intermediate presprint conditioning program   97

Basic sprint program   98
Intermediate sprint program   99
Advanced sprint program 1   100
Advanced sprint program 2   101

Advanced circuit training program   108

Basic preconditioning power program   116
Intermediate preconditioning power program   117

Basic power program   118
Intermediate power program   119
Advanced power program 1   120
Advanced power program 2   122

Sport	Developmental focus of rope jumping	Suggested programs
General fitness	1. Efficiently warms the muscles in the upper and lower body before stretching exercises and weight training 2. Helps develop the aerobic capacity in one third of the time other exercises take 3. Tones and trims legs, gluteals, and waist line 4. Aids in weight loss 5. Serves as a cool-down after exercise to lower respiration 6. Serves as an active rest exercise between weightlifting sets **Recommendation:** Incorporate the high step to work the stomach, firm the buttocks, and shape the legs. The X-foot cross trims inner and outer thigh muscles.	Four-step conditioning program Jump for 10 minutes at 70-80% of MHR Jump for 30 minutes at 60-70% of MHR for weight loss
Injury rehabilitation	Injuries are sometimes the result of muscles and joints being undeveloped, overused, and imbalanced in strength and flexibility. Rope jumping is recommended by many physical therapists as a technique for building endurance and kinesthetic awareness in the lower extremities. **Recommendation:** For rehabilitating injuries occurring in the ankles, feet, and knees first try a lower impact activity such as the stationary bike, swimming, and jogging to build some strength. Then switch to jump rope as a graded exercise for improving proprioception and strength in the feet, ankles, knees, wrists, and shoulders. Aim for low impact, low height, and short contact, and be light on the balls of the feet.	Bounce step: 1-9 reps per set times 5 sets Build up to 100 reps of non-stop jumping Build up to 250 reps Build to 500 reps

Sport	Developmental focus of rope jumping	Suggested programs		
		Off-season	**Preseason**	**In-season**
Body building **Olympic lifting** **Strength training**	1. Improves aerobic fitness. Offsets valsalvic effects imposed upon the heart by squatting and bench pressing 2. Provides heart with rhythmic steady exercise during heavy strength training cycles 3. Improves anaerobic fitness levels to decrease rest time between sets 4. Serves as an effective warm-up, cool-down, and active rest between weightlifting sets 5. Conditions shoulder and leg muscles to aid recovery from lifting **Recommendation:** Jump on nonlifting days. First reach 140 jumps without a miss, then 250 jumps times 2, and then 500 jumps with 10-second interval sprints.	Preparation and intermediate phase in the four-step conditioning program	Conditioning phase in the four-step conditioning program for cardio	Jump for 1 minute between sets Jump 1000 reps times 3 sets using the bounce and alternate-foot steps for aiding in weight loss

t	Developmental focus of rope jumping	Suggested programs		
		Off-season	**Preseason**	**In-season**
Boxing **Ultimate fighting** **Wrestling** **All forms ofmartial arts**	1. Develops hand and foot speed for punching, blocking, throwing, feinting, and leg sweeping movements in offensive and defensive takedown and ground attacks 2. Improves strength development of hip flexors, legs, knees, ankles, and feet for kicking and balancing while throwing, hooking legs, and doing sweeping movements 3. Develops anaerobic energy for matching the high intensity of 3-minute rounds of nonstop fighting and aerobic energy for 12 rounds 4. Develops eye, hand, and foot coordination for proper awareness during landing, punching, kicking, and forearm and knee strikes. 5. Develops good balance and agility in reacting to punches, kicks, takedowns, and throws 6. Develops muscular endurance of the arms, chest, and back for grappling, pulling, punching, blocking, and throwing **Recommendation:** Use full twister, high step, and bounding movements in warm-up programs. Replace technique in sprint programs with the high step and side swing to jump.	Four-step conditioning program Basic and intermediate sprint and power preconditioning programs Basic sprint program (30 sec)	Intermediate and advanced sprint programs (60-120 sec) Basic power program	Advanced sprint programs (90-120 sec) Advanced power programs Advanced circuit training program

Sport	Developmental focus of rope jumping	Suggested programs		
		Off-season	**Preseason**	**In-season**
Gymnastics Cheerleading Dance Ballet	1. Develops the maximal and submaximal vertical leap capability needed for acrobatic and dance movements 2. Develops leg, knee, ankle, and foot strength for repetitive jumping, flipping, spinning, and landing movements 3. Improves endurance and strength of hand and wrist muscles for eagle, over and under grips, and other hand movements **Recommendation:** Incorporate some triple unders in the power programs. Concentrate on proper form and safe landings.	Four-step conditioning program Basic and intermediate sprint and power preconditioning programs	Intermediate sprint program (60 sec) Advanced power programs Advanced circuit training program	Advanced warm-up program

Sport	Developmental focus of rope jumping	Suggested programs		
		Off-season	**Preseason**	**In-season**
Football Rugby Soccer	1. Develops footwork necessary to cover short and long distances very fast while avoiding tackles and obstacles 2. Develops explosive power movements off the line, in the backfield, on kick off and returns, and after quick stops during the course of the game 3. Develops agility for rapid and accurate changes in direction during pass patterns to catch or receive the ball and during running to evade tackles or defenders 4. Develops eye, hand, and foot coordination and body awareness when kicking, catching, or passing the ball 5. Develops speed, quickness, and agility which enables the athlete to assess the game situation and react quickly, while moving at top speed 6. Develops leg, knee, ankle, and foot strength for preventing injuries 7. Develops balance and coordination to maintain body control and posture when moving with or without the ball	Four-step conditioning program Basic and intermediate sprint and power pre-conditioning programs	Basic and intermediate sprint programs (30-60 sec) Basic and intermediate power programs	Advanced warm-up program Advanced circuit training program

Sport	Developmental focus of rope jumping	Suggested programs		
		Off-season	Preseason	In-season
Baseball Softball	1. Develops eye, hand, and foot coordination for hitting, pitching, catching, and throwing the ball 2. Improves aerobic endurance to prevent fatigue in shoulder and arm muscles for hitting, throwing, pitching, and catching 3. Develops high levels of anaerobic fitness for sprinting around bases, catching the ball, or making plays 4. Develops rotational and pivotal hip movements for batting and pitching 5. Improves footwork and agility for reacting instantly to playing situations 6. Improves hand and wrist strength for grabbing, catching, and throwing **Recommendation:** Incorporate arm movements with the arm side swing and arm crossover for hand-eye coordination. Focus on 10-second sprints during jumping.	Four-step conditioning program Basic and intermediate sprint and power pre-conditioning programs	Basic sprint program (30 sec) Advanced circuit training program	Advanced warm-up program

Sport	Developmental focus of rope jumping	Suggested programs		
		Off-season	Preseason	In-season
Tennis Badminton Tabletennis Racquetball Squash	1. Helps develop high levels of aerobic and anaerobic endurance for conditioning muscles of the whole body to help maintain good technique, balance, and body control throughout the game 2. Improves timing, rhythm, and hip and pelvic rotation for striking forces to perform horizontal and vertical swinging actions 3. Improves endurance in hands, wrists, and arms for improved grip and racket control 4. Conditions the legs to perform a series of low-elevation jumps combined with submaximal-elevation jumps for serving, striking, and returning the ball or shuttle 5. Improves hand and foot speed and footwork necessary for recognizing situations and reacting instantaneously during high-intensity play 6. Develops proprioception of ankles and feet to reduce risk of injuries **Recommendation:** Jump for durations of 15-30 minutes to build aerobic capacity. Incorporate the power jump, skier's jump, side straddle, and bell jump.	Four-step conditioning program Basic and intermediate sprint and power preconditioning programs	Intermediate and advanced sprint programs (60-120 sec) Intermediate and advanced power programs	Advanced warm-up program Advanced circuit training program

Sport	Developmental focus of rope jumping	Suggested programs		
		Off-season	Preseason	In-season
Field hockey Lacrosse	1. Improves agility for rapid and accurate directional change in offensive play while avoiding defensive movements 2. Improves body awareness and eye, hand, and foot coordination for striking and throwing objects while moving 3. Develops hand grip, forearm strength, and endurance for racket and stick control 4. Improves endurance in shoulders and arms for striking muscles **Recommendation:** Incorporate some side straddles and X-foot crosses for lateral shifting in the sprint programs.	Four-step conditioning program Basic and intermediate sprint and power preconditioning programs	Intermediate and advanced sprint programs (60-120 sec) Basic power program	Advanced circuit training program

Sport	Developmental focus of rope jumping	Suggested programs		
		Off-season	**Preseason**	**In-season**
Basketball Volleyball Handball	1. Develops eye, hand, and foot coordination, balance, and body awareness for striking, setting, serving, blocking, spiking, dunking, dribbling, and shooting skills 2. Improves agility for quickness on and off the ball while maintaining good form and control 3. Develops proprioception, strength, and endurance in the feet, ankles, knees, and legs for jumping, stopping, starting, pivoting, rotating, lateral movements, and forward and backward movements 4. Reduces impact by using the lower extremities (feet, ankles, knees, legs, hips, and lower back) as a buffer to absorb forces from continuous jumping movements over the course of the game 5. Conditions muscles in the lower body to build leg power and perform a continuous series of quick, explosive, high-elevation jumps 6. Conditions the muscles of the upper body for rotational trunk movements when passing, shooting, and striking 7. Develops wrist and hand strength and endurance for catching, grabbing, dribbling, passing, and striking the ball for long periods of time 8. Improves vertical acceleration **Recommendation:** Perform all foot movements. During power jump programs incorporate the power side straddle, forward straddle, skier's jump, bell jump, and full twister.	Four-step conditioning program Basic sprint program (30 sec) Basic power program	Intermediate and advanced sprint programs (60-120 sec) Intermediate and advanced power programs	Advanced warm-up program Advanced circuit training program

Sport	Developmental focus of rope jumping	Suggested programs		
		Off-season	**Preseason**	**In-season**
Track and field **Sprinting** **Distance running** **Field events**	1. Improves balance and body awareness during running and jumping events 2. Develops explosive first steps for start speed and power off the blocks in running events 3. Develops upper-body momentum for events that involve throwing objects 4. Improves speed by simulating the sprint running step and increases stride length and leg, hip, ankle, and foot strength 5. Develops anaerobic fitness to improve sprint speed and kicking 6. Develops gripping strength and endurance in wrists and hands 7. Develops hand and foot coordination **Recommendation:** The high step is excellent for improving sprinting stride.	Four-step conditioning program Basic and intermediate sprint and power preconditioning programs	Advanced sprint programs (90-120 sec) Advanced power programs Advanced circuit training program	Advanced warm-up program

Sport	Developmental focus of rope jumping	Suggested programs		
		Off-season	**Preseason**	**In-season**
Swimming **Water polo** **Diving** **Synchronized swimming**	1. Develops explosive start speed for pushing off the wall, board, or platform 2. Develops anaerobic fitness for sprinting and endurance in the arms for stroking motions 3. Develops rhythm and timing for better arm strokes 4. Develops endurance in the wrists and hands for grasping the ball for long periods of time 5. Develops upper- and lower-body endurance for stroking motions and treading water for long periods of time **Recommendation:** Focus on developing anaerobic capacity.	Four-step conditioning program Basic and intermediate sprint and power preconditioning programs	Basic and intermediate sprint programs (30-60 sec) Basic and intermediate power programs	Advanced circuit training program

Sport	Developmental focus of rope jumping	Suggested programs		
		Off-season	Preseason	In-season
Ice hockey	1. Develops agility for sudden changes of movement in all directions while assessing the game situation and avoiding opponents 2. Develops explosive start movements 3. Improves hand and foot coordination for striking the puck 4. Improves gripping strength for better stick control 5. Improves hand and foot quickness for offensive and defensive maneuvers while developing foot, ankle, and knee strength 6. Helps maintain balance during the constant shifting of body weight 7. Improves rotational movements for skating and striking the puck	Four-step conditioning program Basic and intermediate sprint and power pre-conditioning programs	Intermediate and advanced sprint programs (60-120 sec) Intermediate and advanced power programs	Advanced warm-up program Advanced circuit training program

Sport	Developmental focus of rope jumping	Suggested programs		
		Off-season	**Preseason**	**In-season**
Figure skating **Synchronized skating** **Inline/roller skating**	1. Improves agility for sudden changes of movement in all directions 2. Develops hand and wrist strength for hand locks and grips during pairs and group routines 3. Develops pivotal and rotational movements for skating, jumping, and spinning 4. Develops aerobic and anaerobic fitness for short and long programs 5. Develops foot, ankle, and knee strength to buffer landing during moderate- to high-elevation jumps and to minimize injuries 6. Improves posture and stabilization of upper and lower body to defer fatigue 7. Improves overall concentration 8. Reduces body fat and increases lean muscle mass 9. Develops quick and efficient movements on the ice	Four-step conditioning program Basic sprint and power preconditioning programs	Basic and intermediate sprint programs (30-60 sec) Basic, intermediate, and advanced I power programs	Advanced warm-up program Basic power program

Sport	Developmental focus of rope jumping	Suggested programs		
		Off-season	Preseason	In-season
Golf **Bowling** **Archery** **Shooting**	1. Conditions muscles of the shoulders, fingers, wrists, and hands for repetitive pulling and swinging movements 2. Improves aerobic fitness for muscle relaxation, rhythm, timing, and controlled breathing during shooting, pulling, and swinging arm movements 3. Develops endurance for maintaining relaxed breathing and concentration through long competition periods 4. Develops eye, hand, and foot coordination, balance, and stability while maintaining good body position and timing for arm and hand releases 5. Develops upper-body stability and balance during movements with an object in the hands **Recommendation:** Build up to 100 jumps without a miss using the bounce step and alternate-foot step. Then build up to 250 jumps times 2 and then to 500 jumps.	Preparation, intermediate, and conditioning phase in the four-step conditioning program	Basic sprint and power preconditioning programs Jump for 10 min at 70-80% of MHR	Basic to advanced warm-up programs

Sport	Developmental focus of rope jumping	Suggested programs		
		Off-season	**Preseason**	**In-season**
Extreme sports	1. Helps develop hand and footwork for reacting to sudden changes in direction while maintaining good balance 2. Develops eye, hand, and foot coordination, concentration, and body control for proper awareness during jumping, leaping, falling, and spinning 3. Develops hand and wrist strength and endurance for grasping for long periods of time 4. Develops endurance for sustaining body control and concentration and maintaining high-performance play 5. Conditions the athlete to perform a series of low- to high-elevation jumps while maintaining body awareness and good balance **Recommendation:** Incorporate all techniques and use all planes (horizontal, lateral). Use the high step in the sprint programs, and all jumps for better balance and agility.	Four-step conditioning program Basic and intermediate power preconditioning programs	Intermediate and advanced sprint programs (60-120 sec) Intermediate and advanced power programs Advanced circuit training program	Advanced warm-up program Basic and intermediate power preconditioning programs

BIBLIOGRAPHY

Chu, Donald A. 1998. *Jumping into plyometrics*. 2nd ed. Champaign, IL: Human Kinetics.

Cook, Gray. 2003. *Athletic body in balance*. Champaign, IL: Human Kinetics.

Cooper, Kenneth R. 1977. *The aerobics way: New data on the world's most popular exercise program*. NY: Bantam Books/M. Evans & Company.

National Strength and Conditioning Association. 2000. *Essentials of strength training and conditioning*. Champaign, IL: Human Kinetics.

Pitreli, John, and Pat O'Shea. 1986. Rope jumping: The biomechanics, techniques of and application to athletic conditioning. *NSCA Journal* 8 (4).

Radcliffe, James C., and Robert C. Farentinos. 1998. *High powered plyometrics*. Champaign, IL: Human Kinetics.

Zarrilli, Phillip B. 1998. *When the body becomes all eyes: Paradigms, discourses, and practices of power in Kalarippayatta, a south Indian martial art*. NY: Oxford University Press.

INDEX

Note: The italicized *f* and *t* following page numbers refer to figures and tables, respectively.

A

aerobic base for endurance
    aerobic conditioning 57-58
    Bobby Fischer 62
    four-step conditioning program
      58-62
agility
    about 103, 104
    circuit training program 107-109
    developing rhythm 104-105
    kinesthetic awareness 105-107
    World Champion and 110
Ali, Muhammad 1
anaerobic fitness, improving
    aerobic vs anaerobic training 65
    avoiding injury 65
    muscle fatigue 65
    preparing for 65
    recovery period 64
    starting 63, 64
    supercompensation principle
      64
anaerobic power
    aerobic vs anaerobic training
      63
    sports training phase 65-67
Angle, Kurt 124-125

B

basic jump capacity 58
biomechanics of rope jumping

flight phase 27, 28, 28*f*
landing phase 28, 29, 29*f*
load phase 27, 27*f*
body position
    balanced and unbalanced 23
    proper grip 24, 24*f*
    shadow jumping 25, 25*f*, 26, 26*f*
    starting position 23, 23*f*

C

circuit training program
    advanced circuit training pro-
      gram 108-109
    prerequisites before starting
      107
    pretest examples 107, 107*t*
competitive edge
    aerobic and anaerobic training 5
    agility 6
    edges in time 4-5
    explosiveness 6, 7
    quickness 6
    speed 5
conditioning program, four-step
    conditioning phase 61
    intermediate phase 60-61
    phases 59
    preparation phase 59-60
    principles of 58
    sports training phase 61-62
    when to use 59

D

Duran, Roberto 1

F

Fischer, Bobby 62

G

Gostigian, Michael 90

H

Han, Kevin 102
hyperformance speed ropes 16, 19

I

ice therapy 35
injury prevention
    about 33
    caring for 35
    causes and precautions 34
    common injuries 35
    proceeding systematically 35
    proper execution, takeoff and
        landing 34
Inside Kung-Fu 19
intensity, measuring
    exceeding baseline 70
    pretest 69-70
    pretest for establishing baseline
        70-72
    target training zones 72
    Weiss, Michael 72

J

jump rope. *See* rope jumping

K

kinesthetic awareness
    developing 106
    missteps and catches 106
    monitoring attention style 106
    neuromuscular coordination
        105
    rope jumping as training activity
        105-106

L

Lee, Bruce 1, 16

Lee, Buddy 102, 124
Leonard, Sugar Ray 1
lightweight speed ropes 15
low-impact jumping: level 1
    arm crossover 51
    arm side swing 52
    backward jumping 50
    backward shuffle 48
    bell jump 43
    forward shuffle 47
    forward straddle 41
    full twister 45
    half twister 44
    heel to toe 49
    high step 39
    repetition of jump, counting 38
    side straddle 40
    side swing to jump 53
    skier's jump 42
    x-foot cross 46

M

Maris, Roger 1
maximal oxygen uptake 3-4
McGwire, Mark 1

P

Pekarek, Justin 110
performance-based (RPM) chart
    intensity chart using alternate-
        foot step 74*t*
    intensity chart using power
        jump 74*t*
    making gains 73-74
plyometrics exercises
    about 112, 113
    benefits 113
    eccentric and concentric con-
        tractions 113-114
    principles of 113
power and explosiveness
    about 111-112
    eccentric and concentric con-
        tractions 113-114
    plyometrics exercises 112, 113
power jumping: level 2

about 54
power jump 55-56
power programs
    advanced power program-1 120-121
    advanced power program-2 122-123
    basic power program 118
    basic preconditioning power program 116
    benefits of 114
    intermediate power program 119
    intermediate preconditioning power program 117
    pretest examples 114, 115*t*
pretest, establishing baseline
    about 70
    benefits 71, 72
    gains 72
    pretest examples 71*t*
    taking 71
proficiency, developing 33, 34

Q

Quick, Richard 11

R

Rauthe, Jorg 92
rhythm
    explained 105
    multijoint training and sense of rhythm 105
    training 104-105
rhythmics 104
Richardson, Burton 16, 19
rope jumping
    competitive edge 4-7
    maximizing 7-8
    sports training potential of 1
rope jumping, benefits
    concentration 3-4
    dynamic balance 2
    maximal oxygen uptake 3-4
    movements, efficient and inefficient 3

neuromuscular adjustments 2, 3
    universal athletic position 2, 2*f*, 3
rope jumping vs exercises
    about 8
    energy expenditure 10*t*-11*t*
    exercise comparison chart 8, 9*t*
    fat-burning calories 9
    running 9
    swimmers 11
rope measurements
    adjusting length 21
    chest measurement 21, 22*f*
    ideal rope length 19
    lower rib cage measurement 21, 22*f*
    shorter rope 19
    standard measurement 20, 20*f*, 21
ropes
    body position 23-26
    care 19
    choosing 15
    continuation 16
    materials, fast-turning and slow-turning 16
    types, comparing 16, 17*t*-18*t*
    for unskilled and skilled jumpers 15-16
rope training, maximizing
    demands of 7
    proficiency, improving 8
Rouse, Jeff 66
Rusli, Ignatius 102

S

shadow jumping
    jumping properly 25, 26
    stages 25, 25*f*, 26*f*
shoes and attire 15
simulation
    about 127
    principles of 127-128
skills, mastering
    biomechanics of rope jumping 27-29

skills, mastering *(continued)*
    body position 23-27
    injury, prevention 33-35
    proficiency, developing 33
    ropes 15-22
    shoes and attire 15
    surface and training area 13-15
    two basic techniques 30-32
Smith, Emmitt 1
Spassky, Boris 62
speed and quickness
    about 91
    hand and foot speeds 91, 92
    sprint training programs, ben-
        efits 91-92, 93
    U.S. national badminton team
        102
sports and fitness goals, condition
        for
    seasonal training cycles 128-132
    simulation, principles of 127-
        128
sport-specific programs
    about 132
    program index 133
    programs 134-148
sports training phase
    intensity level 66
    meeting standard 66, 67
    Rouse, Jeff 66
    10-minute set 65-66
sprint programs
    about 94
    advanced sprint program-1 95,
        100
    advanced sprint program-2 95,
        101
    basic presprint conditioning
        program 95, 96
    basic sprint program 95, 98
    intermediate presprint condi-
        tioning program 95, 97
    intermediate sprint program 95,
        99
sprint programs, preparing
    about 93

alternate-foot step 93
    pretest examples 94, 94*t*
sprint training programs
    benefits of 91, 92, 93
    hand and foot speeds 91
    light on the feet 91, 92
Stearns, Billy 92
strength and power
    Angle, Kurt 124-125
    power and explosiveness 111-
        114
    power programs 114-123
stretching
    about 78
    Achilles stretch 82, 82*f*
    hip adductor stretch 82, 82*f*
    hip flexor stretch 79, 79*f*
    seated hamstrings and calf
        stretch 79, 79*f*
    standing calf stretch 80, 80*f*
    standing hamstrings stretch 80,
        80*f*
    symmetry and asymmetry 78
    torso stretch 81, 81*f*
supercompensation principle 64
surface and training area
    hard and soft surfaces 14
    surfaces, about 13
    training area, about 14, 14*f*, 15

T

target heart rates, chart 73
target training zones, chart 72
techniques, two basic
    alternate-foot step 30, 32
    bounce step 30, 31
training and competing
    intensity level 69
    measuring intensity 69-72
    performance-based RPM 73-74
    target heart rates 73
training cycles, seasonal
    about 128-129
    in-season 131-132
    off-season 129-130
    preseason 130-131

training methods
    about 37
    low-impact jumping: level 1 38-53
    power jumping: level 2 54-56
    problems learning skills 37-38
    sports training jumps, levels of
      38

U

universal athletic position 2, *2f,* 3

V

Von Heiland, Erica 102

W

warming up
    methods 75-76
    procedures 76-77
    starting 76

warming up and cooling down
    about 75
    active rest 77
    cooling down 78
    stretching 78-82
warm-up programs
    about 83
    advanced warm-up program 88-
      90
    basic warm-up program 84-85
    intermediate warm-up program
      86-87
Weisiger, Audrey 110
Weiss, Michael 72, 110
Williams, Walter Ray, Jr. 57
Woods, Tiger 57

ABOUT THE AUTHOR

Buddy Lee, president and founder of Jump Rope Technology, Inc., has fashioned a worldwide reputation with his incredible jump rope skills. He has performed in exhibitions for sports events, presidents, and world leaders in 24 countries.

Lee used rope jumping as a key part of his wrestling training to develop into a world-class and Olympic athlete. He was a 1992 Olympian in Greco-Roman wrestling and a 20-time U.S. national and Armed Forces champion in three different styles of wrestling. After earning a degree in secondary education from Old Dominion University, where he was a two-time NCAA All-American wrestler, he served 11 years in the U.S. Marine Corps, where he became a three-time national champion, a three time World Military champion, and a three-time World Cup and Pan Am medalist. He also was voted outstanding wrestler in the 1992 national wresting championships and was Marine Athlete of the Year twice.

He served as the jump rope conditioning consultant to the U.S. Olympic Committee from 1996 to 2000, training 25 Olympic teams and many gold medalists. Today he consults with the U.S. Professional Tennis Association, the U.S. Figure Skating Association, and several other organizations. Buddy is the co-inventor of the Hyperformance swivel bearing ropes, designed to produce speeds of up to six revolutions per second and eliminate drag and friction present in other ropes. Buddy is also an international motivational speaker and author on rope jumping for several national sport magazines. He travels the country training athletes and fitness enthusiasts with his jump rope system. Buddy resides in Woodbridge, Virginia outside of Washington, D.C.